COMMUNITY ORGANIZATION AND ADULT EDUCATION

Edmund deS. Brunner

COMMUNITY ORGANIZATION AND ADULT EDUCATION

A Five=Year Experiment

With the assistance of: GORDON BLACKWELL · LAURA S. EBAUGH

R. O. JOHNSON · CLARENCE B. LOOMIS · MARGARET CHARTERS LYON

RALPH M. LYON · NICHOLAS MITCHELL

CHAPEL HILL · 1942

THE UNIVERSITY OF NORTH CAROLINA PRESS

Preface

THIS BOOK is a report of a five-year experiment in community organization and development on a county-wide scale in Greenville County, South Carolina. It was initiated July 1, 1936, and ended June 30, 1941. The experiment was made possible by a grant of $80,000 from the General Education Board and by the coöperation of Furman University, a Southern Baptist denominational college, located in the city of Greenville.

The report begins with an account of the conception and initiation of the project and a description of its setting, Greenville County. Chapter II is devoted to the organization and functioning of the County Council for Community Development, through which agency the experiment was conducted. The role of the Council in assisting existing agencies and in organizing new ones is then examined. A fourth chapter tells the story of local community councils. The narrative then turns to the share of the college in the whole enterprise and the degree of success achieved in "getting it off its hill." Next a chapter is given over to the Negro work. The final chapter of conclusions attempts to draw from this experiment certain implications for the field of community organization.

This report would have been impossible without the unstinting coöperation of the staff of the Greenville County Council for Community Development. Each of the staff wrote manuscripts of considerable length dealing with his own activities in the work of the Council. Most of them frankly appraised their successes and their mistakes. All of them read and criticized this report to its benefit. One member of the staff, Dr. Margaret Charters Lyon, collected this material and developed a detailed outline for a book of considerable size. This was invaluable in the preparation of this report.

The executive secretary of the Greenville County Council for Community Development, Mr. Clarence Black Loomis, was also indispensable in the completion of this task. He wrote, in addition to participating in the above process, the reports on the work done by staff members who left the project before the five-year period was over. Mr. Loomis has under way a book which examines the existing sociological theories of community organization in the light of the Greenville experience. The present writer has had free access to that manuscript. It will be a most valuable companion volume to the present report.

The author of this report has not approached his task unacquainted with the experiment or its locale. For the duration of the project he served as its consultant and spent many days in the county, meeting with the staff and committees of the Council itself and in accompanying staff members to their assignments in all of the county's sub-regions.

This fact is both an asset and a liability. It has given the writer an intimate view of the process he now essays to describe and in part to analyze. By the same token, however, it has deprived him of some degree of objectivity. It has made criticism the more difficult for he has been perhaps too conscious of extenuating circumstances in some of the mistakes and of the achievements that in many particulars seemed to overbalance the failures.

The report, however, contains some analysis and therefore some criticism. No project like the Greenville County Council for Community Development can exist for five years and not make mistakes, both minor and serious. The members and staff of the County Council would be the last to wish these glossed over, for it is their hope—a hope born of talking to hundreds who came to study the experiment while it was in process—that no inconsiderable share of whatever good may accrue from the project may be in the help it brings to others outside the county who are interested in community organization. This indeed was one of the motives behind the supporting grant.

The present reporter wishes to emphasize that for this criticism he takes full responsibility. No present or former member of the staff shares in that responsibility in any way. It is hoped that the staff and those people of Greenville County who may chance to read this report will feel that the appraisal of success and failure has been as fairly meted out as the writer believes it has been. If there has been failure in this or any other respect it is also hoped that it will be treated with that high degree of consideration which has made working with the people of the county in the Greenville County Council for Community Development these last five years a very real pleasure.

EDMUND DES. BRUNNER

CONTENTS

COMMUNITY ORGANIZATION AND
ADULT EDUCATION

CHAPTER I

The Project and Its Setting

FOR THE LAST five years Greenville County, South Carolina, has been the locale of a unique effort designed to help an entire county and its communities and neighborhoods to lift themselves by their own bootstraps.

It has long been recognized that life in the twentieth century was a complex affair, replete with adjustments, needs, and problems growing out of the impact of world forces and technological and social inventions upon the simpler and largely agrarian culture of most of the previous century.

It has also been recognized that necessary adjustments were made slowly; that social efforts to meet problems that arose grew in piecemeal fashion; that as a result while some needs, such as for the education of children, were met with reasonable effectiveness, others were neglected, inefficiently coped with, or became the interest of competitive groups or agencies. The amount of social waste inherent in the average community as a result of this situation has grown to impressive proportions.

In 1936 Greenville County set about seeing what it could do by way of marshaling its assets more effectively through community organization and adult education to meet some of its needs and solve some of its problems. It believed it had in its existing organizations and institutions, in its people and their leaders, in its soil, scenery and industries, the ingredients for a better level of living if these could be organized more effectively. Its interests were as wide as the basic human activities of getting a living, making homes, educating youths and adults, using leisure well, improving health, strengthening religion, helping the disadvantaged and governing efficiently.

It was an ambitious program. Its mistakes and failures no less than its achievements have significance for those engaged in what has come to be called inclusively and a bit loosely, community organization. Perhaps in these dark years what went on in Greenville County as the clouds of world revolution gathered into the hurricane of world war has special value. For only by the courageous, efficient, and economic utilization and organization of all its resources can the essential essence of the social gains of nearly two centuries of national life be preserved in the communities of the land in some one of which all live, move, and have their being and experience the impact of social and economic forces and the workings of democracy.

This enterprise in Greenville County, known as the Greenville County Council for Community Development, whatever else it did and was, was in essence also and chiefly an effort to make democracy function; and its knowledge and definition of democracy, though never stated in so many words, changed and developed as the work progressed.

By some canons the very organization of the Council was not democratic. No large number of the people of Greenville County asked for it. But one of the privileges of democracy is that any citizen can propose an idea that seems good to him, that he can attempt to sell it in the market place of public opinion where in a free country all ideas for proper social action compete for the support of free men. In that sense the Council followed the democratic pattern.

Its initial form was no one individual's idea. A university professor had proposed that in various types of communities, with the coöperation of local agencies and outside experts, integrated surveys covering the major areas of human life and interest be made to determine possible and practical programs, that the local agencies attempt by education and action to carry out these programs, that after annual check-ups for from seven to ten years a resurvey be made to measure achievement and evaluate the possibilities of education broadly conceived in coöperation with action agencies, producing desired social change. It was too costly a proposal to secure support. A graduate student in his dissertation proposed and then sought financing for a detailed program for adult education in southern cotton mill villages intended to improve the condition of the workers by applying new knowledge to their daily living. A denominational college president was anxious to find some way of getting his students off their hill and into contact with life so that learning might have practical or at least experimental testing in the crucible of community living. A school administrator had achieved an excellent record in making the curriculum of his schools more functional in terms of the socio-economic setting of his district and wished help to expand the work further. The two last both worked in Greenville County. All four approached the same foundation—the General Education Board. It seemed possible to combine these projects with considerable adaptation, and a grant was made to the to-be-formed Greenville County Council for Community Development which the Board announced in its Annual Report for 1935-6 as follows:

The proposal embraced education from the kindergarten through adulthood; library service, public health and social service, economic stability, cultural advantages, interracial understanding, rural-urban coöperation, unified administrative direction, and a training ground for students of three or more institutions of higher learning in the actual experiences of life in these activities. It represented a type of community experimentation for the purposes of realizing such better understanding and use of available resources as the report of the regional study[1] strongly advocated. The Board made an appropriation of $80,000.00 to the Greenville County Council for Community Development to aid its demonstration over a five-year period on a diminishing scale, with the expectation that the community will gradually take over and continue the support of the services established.

This volume is the story of what happened to the Council and the County in the five-year period of the experiment. But before beginning that story it is important to describe Greenville County and its people.

GREENVILLE COUNTY

The selection of Greenville County was a happy one. Located at the northwest corner of South Carolina it projects southward for 52 miles with a median width of 20 miles. It is not too much to say that within its 800 square miles the county illustrates many of the conditions and important problems of the South. Its three northern townships lie within the Blue Ridge Mountains. Well forested, the farms are small with seldom better than "fair" land. The people, numbering 5,200, live in coves and their habits and mores are typical of the Appalachian highlands. The population of this area gained over 50 per cent between 1930 and 1940. Only 8 per cent of the inhabitants of this region of the county are Negro.

Just south of these lie the four townships of the second region. Here over 90 per cent of the 12,500 people live on small farms, largely as owner-operators. Many of these farms have been taken from the forests within the memory of the people now living on them so that some of the experiences of pioneering have entered into the life of this area. The soil, which is "fair" to "good," still supports small and scattered stands of timber. Just under one fifth of the

1. I.e., Howard W. Odum, *Southern Regions*, University of North Carolina Press, 1936.

population are Negroes. Population in this area increased 25 per cent in the 1930's.

The third region of two townships contains the county-seat city of Greenville and its surrounding area of textile mills and villages, in effect a single metropolitan area though containing a growing number of part-time farmers on small tracts. Nearly 96,000 people live here, slightly more than one fifth Negroes. Main arteries of steam and highway transportation run through the center of this region.

The southern half of the county makes up the fourth and last region. It is divided into seven townships. The population of over 27,700 is 80 per cent farm, one third Negro. It has not shared in the county's population gain, growing only less than 5 per cent in the last census period. Its primary services are performed in several villages. Most of the tenant-operated farms and practically all of the county's sharecroppers are in this region. Farm acreage is larger than elsewhere in the county; soils run from "poor" to "good."

It will be judged from this brief description that it is in the similarity of its diverse regions to certain well-recognized types of areas within the South, rather than its statistical averages for the county as a whole, that Greenville may be said to have a representative character. The County Council had to vary its approach and program significantly in these various areas. But while this is true a closer acquaintance with the county as a whole is essential to a better understanding of the project.

Even a cursory study of census facts relating to Greenville County and city indicates that it varies in many ways from average conditions in South Carolina, and in most cases the divergences from the state average are factors that can be put down on the credit side.

Population changes.—South Carolina is changing only slightly from a rural to a more urbanized state. Fifty years ago 90 per cent of the population was rural and even in 1940 the figure was 75.5 as against 78.6 per cent in 1930.

Greenville County is 27.2 per cent urban, 2.3 points more than in 1930. Of that three quarters of the population which is rural, about three fifths, 57 per cent, is rural non-farm or village. This is a clear indication, of course, of the industrial composition of the county, but it indicates that a county program must deal with two distinct and somewhat divergent rural groups. In the Parker School district in the textile mill section of the metropolitan area and perhaps in other points, excellent approaches to this situation have been made, but the experience nationally and in Greenville is that an industrial but rural population presents peculiar problems.

In common with a number of Southern states, South Carolina has changed from a predominantly Negro to a predominantly white population, a change which has taken place almost exclusively in the last thirty years when the proportion of whites rose from 44.8 per cent in 1910 to 54.3 in 1930 and 57.2 in 1940. For urban South Carolina in the same years the proportion of whites increased from 54.7 to 62.7. Even in rural areas the same trend is manifest, the increase being from 42 to 55.1 per cent.

Greenville County is out of line with the state on this point, 76.2 per cent of the population being white in 1930 and 77.7 in 1940. This again is one of the indications of industrialization, since the Negro has not to any extent been permitted to compete with the whites in the textile industry. This means, of course, that the Negro population is considerably more of a minority group than is usual in the state.

South Carolina is one of the states which is growing very slowly. The rate of increase between 1910-1930, 14.7, is less than half the rate of increase for the nation as a whole, but in these same years Greenville County added 71 per cent to its population and the city 85 per cent. Greenville township, which contains most of the industrial development, grew even more rapidly between 1920 and 1930. Half the growth of the entire state in this twenty-year period is accounted for by the increased population of Greenville County. Between 1930 and 1940 the state increase was 9.3 per cent against the nation's 7.2 per cent, and the county gained 16.7 per cent.

Age distribution.—It is not at all certain that this rapid increase in population will continue, particularly if the industrial development should no longer be expanded. It seems quite evident that the declining birth rate, which has become pronounced throughout the nation, has begun to take effect in Greenville. This is shown by an analysis of the age distribution of the population. The relatively small number of children under 5 years of age stands out in the table below. Moreover, the number of children under one year of age at the time of the 1930 census was only 18 per cent of the total number under 5 instead of about 21.0 as would be normal in the period before the decline of the birth rate. Interestingly enough the decline in the birth rate, evidenced by these figures, is a characteristic of the urban and rural farm population groups, but not of the rural-non-farm where there are no indications of decline.

AGE DISTRIBUTION OF SELECTED POPULATION GROUPS

Age Groups	State 1930	State 1940	Greenville County 1930	Greenville County 1940	Greenville (city) 1930	Greenville (city) 1940
Under 5	11.8	11.1	11.1	9.5	8.4	7.1
5-9	13.8	11.3	12.9	9.8	10.0	7.2
10-14	12.8	11.4	11.6	10.3	9.1	8.4
30-44	16.7	17.9	18.5	20.9	22.6	23.5
65 and over	3.3	4.2	3.0	3.8	3.5	4.2

This table shows that the tendencies mentioned are more pronounced in the city of Greenville than either county or state. It also indicates that an unusually large proportion of the population are in the years of highest accomplishment of productivity.

Size of family.—The implication of these figures is made all the greater by an examination of the data on the size of families. For the state of South Carolina the average native white urban family consisted in 1930, of 3.77 persons and the Negro family of 3.27. In Greenville city the average white family consists of 3.55 and the Negro 2.78. Practically three fifths of the families in the city of Greenville have no children under 10 years of age.

This may indicate if these trends continue that the city of Greenville will face increasing enrollments in the upper grades and in high schools for some time to come, but that a decreasing enrollment will probably begin to make itself felt in the elementary school in a few years. It is also interesting to note that while the proportion of aged is not high, it has begun to increase, and in 1940 3.8 per cent of the population were 65 years of age and over as against 3.0 per cent in 1910. If this trend continues it may definitely affect the public health program and the adult education program, and it may also begin to color the general level of interest in and concern about community affairs.

School attendance.—In the matter of school attendance Greenville County and city make a sharply better showing than the state as a whole. In the matter of illiteracy Greenville County and city make a better record in the state both among the whites and the Negroes.

SCHOOL ATTENDANCE: 1930

Age Groups	State	Greenville County	Greenville (city)
7-13	86.4	93.1	95.1
14-15	73.8	72.3	78.4
16-17	46.7	44.2	54.0
18-20	18.1	18.0	23.2

ILLITERACY

	State	Greenville County	Greenville (city)
White	5.2	2.8	1.1
Negro	26.9	24.1	19.2

The better record in the years of voluntary school attendance usually indicates an above-average economic situation and this, indeed, characterizes Greenville as compared with the rest of the state.

Retail sales: an index of economic status.—Evidence of this is seen first of all in figures for per capita retail sales. Almost one tenth of the retail stores in South Carolina were in Greenville County—nearly 1,100 both in 1930 and 1933. This had increased to 1,358 stores in 1940, about 7 per cent of the state total. Only one county has more stores and no county has higher gross retail sales. Nearly one half of the county stores are in Greenville, although only a little more than one fourth of the population lives in this city.

In 1929 per capita retail sales in South Carolina were $167; in the county, $272; and in the city of Greenville, $772. This indicates, of course, that much of the county's trade in both these areas is done in the county seat city, but even the county figures show that Greenville is considerably better off than the state as a whole. Measured by this particular index, the county's relative position improved despite the depression, if one can judge from the 1933 Census of Retail Distribution. In the nation as a whole the decline in retail sales was 49 per cent. In South Carolina it was 38 per cent. In Greenville County, 34 per cent. Relative to the state and nation, Greenville was not suffering as severely at the time that this census was undertaken. The per capita retail sales in Greenville County in the latter period amounted to $167; in the city, $528. In other words, Greenville sales in the fiscal year preceding the 1933 Census of Distribution amounted to only slightly less on the per capita basis than those of a comparable city in an adjoining county in 1929. In 1939 South Carolina's trade was better than 1929, $174 per capita. Greenville County also rose slightly to $278, but the city itself lost a little, the figure being $749.

It is quite evident that in comparison with the state, and indeed with much of the South, Greenville has a favored economic position.

Another indication of the economic strength of Greenville is to be found in the average value of homes in 1930. Those of the white owners averaged $5,225 in 1930. On the other hand, less than one third of Greenville County's non-farm homes are owned by their occupants and the rental value of the others is less than $10 a month for both whites and Negroes. This may mean poor housing, but more probably indicates a generous rental policy on the part of the major textile concerns in the mill villages.

In the city of Greenville itself, the value of the homes owned by native whites was $7,800 and the median rental was $26.

Occupational status.—Another index of the character of the community is to be found in the occupation figures. In the United States 40 per cent of the entire population was gainfully employed in 1930 and in South Carolina the average was within half a per cent of the national figure. In Greenville city, however, 48.7 of the population were gainfully employed. This exceeds the New York State average of 44 per cent and probably is one of the explanations of the relatively strong economic position of the city of Greenville as witnessed by the retail sales and the value of the homes owned.

It is interesting to analyze some of the major occupational groups. This is done in the table below. It will be noticed that textiles furnish the greatest amount of employment, though the proportion is not as high as in some textile centers because Greenville has kept the textile industry out of the city limits to a considerable extent. This may be one of the explanations for some of the other comparisons made above. Greenville city is more concerned with trade, banking, real estate, insurance. A higher proportion of her population is engaged in the professions—a factor which is sometimes taken as a measure of community standards.

PROPORTION EMPLOYED IN IMPORTANT OCCUPATION GROUPS: 1930

	South Carolina	Greenville County	Greenville (city)
Per cent total population employed ...	39.5	41.2	48.7
Per cent of employed in textiles	11.5	28.7	7.0
Per cent of employed in trade, banks, real estate, insurance and public services	8.5	12.3	24.0
Per cent of employed in other professions	3.8	4.7	9.2

Agriculture.—It has already been indicated that agriculture is important in Greenville County, but its importance is declining both actually and relatively. In South Carolina the number of farms declined 13 per cent between 1930 and 1940, but the total value increased slightly. In Greenville County in this period the number of farms dropped from 7,079 to 5,607 or 20.8 per cent, and values fell from about $23,250,000 to $16,400,000 or 29.3 per cent. The average value per farm in South Carolina in 1940 was $2,461 or $60 above the 1930 figure. In Greenville County it was $2,932, which though significantly above the state average was nonetheless $353 below the county's 1930 figure. Whereas the farm land increased about one million acres in the 1930's in South Carolina, it declined about 45,000 acres or over thirteen per cent in the county.

Greenville County, like many in this general area of the South, seems to be entering a cycle similar to that of New England sixty or seventy years ago. Then New England agriculture felt the competition of the broad, fertile acres of the Mid-West and rapidly declined, to recover somewhat only when it changed its scheme of farm management from general farming to specialized crops, especially such as helped to feed its rapidly growing manufacturing cities. Similarly

Greenville County has been a cotton county—though with more diversification than many—but its small farms, with their high cost of production, can no longer meet the competition of the cotton Southwest. The impending changes in farm management that may be forced by this situation have not yet gained much headway, for cotton culture is a social system as well as a commercial enterprise. These facts lend point to the agricultural program of the County Council for Community Development, described later.

This decline in Greenville County's farms fell with disproportionate force upon the Negroes, the number of whose farms declined 38.6 per cent in the 1930's as compared to a white loss of 13.8 per cent. Thus in 1930, 28 per cent of the farms were Negro operated but in 1940 only 21.8 per cent. The area of the decline can be made clearer by two other comparisons. The number of sharecroppers dropped sharply, as it did all over the state, from 1,059 in 1930 to 592 in 1940, or 44.1 per cent. The decline in the state was 28.6 per cent. The farms under twenty acres in size in Greenville County declined from 1,731 to 1,081 between 1930 and 1940, or 37.5 per cent. The state loss was ten points less.

These data must not obscure the fact that agriculture in Greenville County is still a considerable enterprise with certain elements of strength. As already indicated the county's farms are worth considerably more on the average than those in the state, despite the fact that their average size is 52.3 acres as against 81.7 acres for the whole state. The 1930 figures were 47.8 and 65.8 acres respectively. Farm ownership by the operators had increased in the county in the 1930's. In 1940 48.5 per cent of the holdings were operated by their owners as against 37.3 per cent in 1930. Indeed the number of owner-operators actually gained 10 per cent in the decade 1930-1940 as against a decline in tenants of almost 35 per cent.

One possible explanation for some of the strengths of the agricultural situation in the county and for the fact that almost one fifth of the farms are less than twenty acres, despite the small proportion of sharecroppers, lies in the opportunity in the county for wage work off the farm offered by the textile mills. Thus 27.3 per cent of Greenville County farmers worked off their farms an average of 137 days in 1939, almost as large a proportion as in 1934, whereas in the state as a whole the proportion was only 23.3 per cent compared to 33.8 per cent in 1934.

Cultural patterns.—Generally speaking, Greenville is of the New, rather than the Old South. This is not to say that it does not have traditions and is not "Southern." However, it differs noticeably from the South's older cities and is perhaps more progressive. Dating its rise to importance in the state back some fifty years only, fewer ante-bellum culture traits are evident in 1941 than is true in longer established Southern centers.

True, the place of the Negro in the community does not depart from the usual Southern caste pattern, but the sporadic activities of the Ku Klux Klan are frowned upon by the community in general. Greenville boasts one of the few Negro urban community centers with a well-rounded program in the South, and local Negro leaders hold a place of respect among the citizens. The fact that the community is Southern indicates that community improvement efforts will have more hope of success if racial lines are followed.

Class lines are fairly definitely recognized, especially as far as the upper economic brackets are concerned. Shot through all economic relationships prevails an attitude of paternalism carried over from the plantation to the textile mill and other employment situations. This is a basic culture trait sometimes hindering democratic community development.

Greenville is characterized by civic pride and push, perhaps more than is true in many Southern towns. Community efforts toward economic development of the city and county are well supported. Less thought is given to coöperative improvement for all the residents. Essentially, the point of view is individualistic.

CHAPTER II

Planning and Functioning of the Council

AMONG THE PEOPLE and under the conditions described, the project outlined on page five was set up in 1936 after much preliminary conference among those interested. Few in the county knew anything about it until the announcement of the grant was made, but the county officials did know and had confidence in the chief local leaders who launched the enterprise.

The county, too, was not devoid of effective agencies at the time the Council was organized. There was a Community Chest in the city which brought about a dozen agencies into coöperation. There was a county library, including, of course, service to the city. Agricultural and Home Economics Extension had been organized for years under the familiar pattern of relationship with the State Agricultural College. These and other agencies too numerous to catalogue were at work, largely within the Greenville metropolitan area. The familiar plaint of the urban center being over-organized was heard. It was natural for the Council then to express its general purposes in terms of coördination and community organization.

This chapter relates to the initial planning of the Council and its mode of functioning. Later chapters will be concerned with the major phases of the Council's work.

The idea of community coördinating councils has been familiar in the United States for 30 years at least. Under the Council of National Defense in 1917-1918 over 4,000 were set up with the view of coördinating various local war-work activities. Ever since there have been those who urged this general form of organization in order to secure a maximum use of local resources and to reduce duplication and waste to a minimum through coördinated planning. Many special interests had over the years organized local councils of social work, health, and adult education, or federations such as those of women's clubs and Protestant churches. Increasingly, too, the implicit concept of planning for social action by such groups had become explicit in their statements and actions. It was upon this general background that the Greenville County Council for Community Development sought to build.

It was apparent at the outset that there were three rather different conceptions of the possibilities and program of the Council. The fanfare of publicity with which the enterprise was announced by the Greenville city press gave the public only a vague idea that money was available for undefined enterprises in community improvement. Proposals flooded in, for the establishment of a municipal orchestra, for building a civic center and a needed new library building, to help the Art League or Drama Guild and so on. Most of those who expressed themselves had in mind a particular need or problem in which coöperative endeavor and the outside funds could be well used. Few, if any, saw the possibilities of an organization to examine and work with all phases of community life.

A second viewpoint was that of the president of the local denominational college, who became president of the Council, and the few of his faculty who had been closest to the planning of the college's share in the program. In this view the Council would function through the social sciences and the arts and to a limited extent through surveys to eventuate in action programs.   An interchange of talents was envisaged; a successful truck farmer might teach urban men to raise vegetables, a wealthy, talented, urban musician might play before rural groups. The needed coördination of the health services might be accomplished. So far as possible the college students would be brought into the program. Beyond this the president properly asked the people of the county to tell the Council what they wanted.

The third viewpoint expressed the professional attitude toward community organization and improvement. It was concerned with helping existing groups to function better, each in its own sphere, and together in an attack on unmet needs; with discovering all the assets and problems; with effective coördination.

There was then at the outset a curious conglomeration of ideas. Even those who sponsored specific proposals did not know the procedures for carrying them out within the type of organization the Council was designed to become under the grant. It gradually became clear that the techniques for solving problems or developing communities had to be evolved. Much of the first two years was spent in resolving different and sometimes conflicting ideas and in making theory concrete.

Initial steps in organization.—These differences and conflicts were not, of course, with respect to the necessity and desirability of having a Council. That had been settled at a preliminary meeting in the early spring of 1936 when 24 persons from 23 institutions, agencies, and organizations in the county met to form the body that should receive the fund if granted. It voted unanimously, "That there was need in Greenville County for a definite effort which would offer opportunity for growth among the people along cultural and technical lines; for coördination of existing agencies; for increasing community pride and spirit; for fostering community enterprise throughout the county; for development of consciousness of the significance of social problems."

These are worthy objectives though general in their statement. They primarily concern adults. They involve for achievement a continuous program of adult education. The very needs expressed are testimony to the fact that democracy as a way of life is rarely established completely in any community. Democracy and coöperation are processes that come to be understood only by practice over the years.

When then it came to implementing this statement of purpose it was small wonder that there was groping for places to take hold. Laymen and professionals, quite effective in their specific areas of interest and responsibility, found themselves baffled as they faced the problems of a county and discovered their lack of acquaintanceship with the varied aspects of its total life.

Stress was laid at the first Council meeting after the grant was made upon the necessity for coördination, but even those who waxed eloquent on the theme grew silent as to what first steps should be taken. After all, the Council had been started. Would not this of itself help coördination as it functioned? There was recognition of the need for a factual basis upon which to act. Others felt an urge to "do something" quickly to gain prestige for the Council. Attention was called to the fact that at the end of the five-year period of the grant "the project should carry itself." But a group puzzled about tomorrow could not think in terms of six years in the future. Finally broad areas of interest and need were mentioned such as health, rural education, recreation, adult education, and general culture. Some of these were discussed and agency representatives offered coöperation.

As was wholly natural, questions of relationship were raised. Was this new Council, known as yet to few in the county but well financed, going to assume the coördinating leadership? Was the leadership of the local college president going to give to his institution control of the program? Again and again through the first years, but with decreasing frequency, it had to be stated that the funds had not been allocated to the college or to any agency in the county but to the Council setup, after full explanation to the representatives of 23 local agencies who had requested the grant. It was also stated at this first Council meeting "that no plans had been made." In a sense this should have been apparent from the meeting itself for certainly no program was handed down or even suggested, to the impatience of a few who demanded "what do you want *us* to do?" On the other hand, a staff was already forming. The "Education Director" and the "Activities Director" had been appointed and were present at the meeting.

The Council ended its first meeting by committing its considerable agenda of unsolved problems to an Executive Committee. Its members doubtless decided to allow the future to determine the question of relationships and act accordingly as the answer to that dilemma emerged.

In retrospect it is easy to say that this matter of the Council's organization could have been more skillfully managed. More persons might have been consulted, more agencies brought in, more time spent in educating and in planning. But those who acted spent untold hours in what preparation was made. The psychological moment seemed to have arrived to secure the foundation grant for something which all who were consulted agreed "would be a good thing." Busy men were carrying the preliminary stages of the organization. To do the job properly would almost have required the services of the very sort of agency they were seeking to set up. They were not only sincere, they were accurate when they said that beyond the general ideas already noted they "had no plans." Certainly many a social enterprise has been launched on its career with far less adequate preparation or participation from those likely to be most concerned. The availability of the funds was a prod to quicker action than might have been the case if the 24 individuals who originally voted to receive the grant if given had been forced, out of their own enthusiasm for the idea, to bring the agencies and individuals of the county into a County Council self-propelled and locally financed from the start.

For the first three months after this meeting the Executive Committee convened weekly to examine various areas of life in Greenville County and to make tentative plans. The health setup was described and one member outlined a plan for coördination. Representatives of recreation agencies reported to the committee and made several suggestions and requests. The head of the Negro Center sat in on a meeting and told of her work. Two colored assistants, a nurse and a recreation leader, were given to the Negro Center by the County Council almost immediately. The Executive Committee also acted upon staff needs and selections. Fortunately, this organization period came in the summer when committee members' own loads were light. As fall pressure began and a staff assembled, the committee asked to be relieved of so many meetings. They played an important part, however, in the early clarification of problems and procedures and continued to function.

Staff.—Before November 1, 1936, the roster of staff had been completed. In addition to the two persons already mentioned, there was a specialist in government, one in arts and crafts, and another in public health. Several members of the faculty of the college, including both sociologists and the head of the department of education, accepted full staff membership. Others, especially in economics and dramatics, participated on certain projects. In each case the professors joined the staff not through any pressure but because of a genuine interest in the work. Practically all the specially employed staff members also did some teaching. Two were paid partly by the Council and partly by the college. With the growth of the staff a coördinator was employed, the term being carefully chosen to indicate that the function of this person was not mainly that of a director or executive secretary but one of coördination and coöperation. In 1938 a Negro coördinator was added.

Not long after the organization of the Council its very existence and function enabled its officers to secure staff assistance from public and private agencies. The National Park Service sent a landscape architect who spent nearly a year in making a recreation study and who incidentally gave advice to schools and community centers in landscaping grounds. A librarian and clerical assistant were provided by the WPA education project. The Macy Fund made three public health nurses available for a demonstration project, and the State Board of Health furnished supervision for this project and the health work of the Council. A recreation institute was made possible through the National Recreation Association, and a specialist in recreation was loaned to the Council by the WPA. In each case the services were well received and the temporary staff members made a contribution to the total program while they were carrying out the jobs to which their national organization had assigned them. In some years the value of services and grants made available by outside agencies equaled more than the basic foundation grant for the year.

Not all of the staff remained with the Council for the entire period. A few mistakes were made in selection, in part because the Council needed people quickly and lacked as clear an understanding as it later gained of the needs and qualifications of each position. Most of the staff were selected by the college president who, because of the planned relationship between the Council and the college, had to have regard for their teaching qualifications.

With the present movement for greater service by colleges to their communities the experience of this project at this point may be of value. It is not easy to be an academician and a community leader at the same time. Some good teachers disliked the drudgery connected with working with informal groups, the uncertainty of attendance, the infinite patience required in leading people to discuss their problems and to work together in solving them. Conversely, good community leaders grew impatient with academic requirements and the details of class procedure. The one group begrudged the time taken from preparation and writing by field work; the other preferred field work to preparation for class responsibilities. The members of the staff varied in the degree of their adjustment to these conflicting demands. Not more than two or three so arranged matters as to be wholly satisfied themselves or wholly to please both the Council and the college. But each person's own decisions were in the main accepted and respected by the others concerned. It is the more surprising, in view of this dilemma, that staff changes were few. The Negro coördinator was the most carefully selected of any staff member. Qualifications were set up and the field canvassed for several months before his appointment.

The task of coördinating the total program required superhuman qualifications. No person was found who could meet every specification. A man who could handle a specialized professional staff, work well with all types of citizens, who had practical experience in administration and group work, and at the same time had a firm footing in the theory of adult education and community procedure, who could teach college courses, and be equally at home in drawing room, farm, or mill village probably does not exist. In 1936 no such list of qualifications as the above was drawn up; the executive committee did not know exactly what kind of person they wanted. The second coördinator appointed in the second year probably combined as many of the requisites as any one person could. Many of the same qualities were needed in other staff members, especially those with large field work responsibilities.

If the Community Council movement grows in the United States a new profession will emerge with its own specific requirements. The Greenville County Council was fortunate in the experience, background, and training of its permanent staff. They were not perfect. They made mistakes. But they were educators in the broad sense of the term. Most of them believed in coöperation and the democratic process. They could discuss rather than quarrel over divergent points of view, especially after the first year. They were willing to experiment. They had had some training in sociology. They liked people. Such qualities are essential.

Volunteer staff.—Early in the fourth year of the County Council's history a step was taken which increased the degree of inter-agency coördination in the county. This was the adding to the staff on an unpaid basis the executives or other professional workers of most of the county-wide agencies. This brought 14 persons into staff relationship. With a few, the step simply recognized what had already taken place. With others the new step made little difference in a nominally coöperative relationship but it signalized a recognition of the need for coördination. In addition the staff consisted in this and the fifth year of ten persons, one assigned by the WPA, one paid jointly by the County Board of Education and the Council, one by the local college and the Council, three professors assigned part time by the college, three drawing their salaries solely from the Council, and one former staff member, married, on a part-time volunteer basis. Two other faculty members gave time occasionally on specific projects. The very fact that this could be accomplished is an evidence of some progress by the Council along the line of one of its major objectives.

Membership in Council.—The first people who gathered together and constituted themselves the Greenville County Council for Community Development were invited in by the two citizens of the county who from the first had helped in formulating the plan and in securing the funds. They were important agency or organization officers with wide connections. They added others and these still others, sometimes rather casually. The general idea was to secure important people from the various sections and major interests in the county up to about 100 persons. At the second meeting of the Council 42 persons gathered classified as follows: Arts 1, Business 4, Education 12, Government 6, Health 8, Religion 1, Rural areas 7, Clubs 3. As the work progressed and local community councils were organized in many parts of the county the membership base broadened from invitation to a ready inclusion of all who accepted responsibilities in the developing program.

This procedure violated the canons of community organization. The Council was neither a federation of agencies nor inclusive of all citizens. The local councils, described later, theoretically met this latter requirement. The County Council was never wholly democratic, but before its five-year period was over the staff saw a prominent citizen of the city who had declared at the first meeting that the people of one section were "barely human" participate in a lively panel discussion with an officer of a local council in this section.

Had the Council from the first sought to build a broad membership base, had it collected even small dues, its continuing program after the grant expired might have been launched on a broader, better-financed basis. But farmers and textile mill workers in the 1930's, with incomes averaging less than $1,000 per year, and Southern Highlanders with even less, had little money to put into such an enterprise. Moreover, with its well-publicized grant the reason for a membership fee would have been difficult to explain. The test of continuing interest and service was therefore, rightly or wrongly, made the basis of membership. This procedure would have been impossible without the grant. By the end of the five-year period the Council had some 200 members. The effort was made throughout to keep the organization as informal and flexible as possible. Articles of Procedure (see Appendix II) were adopted rather than constitution and by-laws.

Council meetings.—The early meetings of the County Council illustrated quite clearly not only the search for procedures and programs but a more fundamental failure to understand the function of discussion in democratic planning. Indeed, some distrusted the process and perhaps its basic objective.

The first annual meeting helped to change this and gave an encouraging example of thinking on county-wide problems. The six committees organized during this year had had from one to a dozen meetings. Each reported to the Council and then after lunch met to consider further steps, augmented by recruits from the Council membership not yet having committee responsibility. The discussion was quite lively in most groups. Each finally reported back to the whole Council. The outcomes of this meeting were uneven. Some committees worked along the lines laid down, some lapsed and had to be resuscitated. It had resulted in an attendance of 80 per cent of the members and in 29 recommendations. Some of these were quite general but a number were definite and formed a basis for work. Later meetings received progress reports and sharpened the recommendations in the light of experience.

Toward the end of the third year a stereopticon slide report of what the Council had done was presented with a discussion of each major area and of next steps. Against this background an important federal officer, a Southerner, spoke on "The South, the Nation's No. 1 Opportunity—IF."

Incidentally, this picturization of the Council's work aroused great interest and was repeated to service clubs and a number of other organizations.

Increasingly at these meetings representatives and reports from the area councils began to be heard.

The close of the third year was marked by a meeting which evidenced the greater degree of coördination slowly emerging among county-wide agencies. There were demonstrations and reports from a dozen such organizations. The Council itself was barely mentioned at this meeting, a real evidence of some measure of success.

Another meeting was held in the county with a most successful local council (see Chapter V) as host and demonstrator. The Governor of the State spoke. Other meetings took up special topics such as youth.

The procedures just outlined had real value. The meetings were held at various points in the county. Instead of the original two and one-half to three hours they took seven, including a social meal, usually outdoors except in fall and winter. The attendance was much better than under the former system. Many more members participated on the program. It should be added that over the whole period of the experiment just over 10 per cent of the present membership never attended a meeting though, when queried, only one fourth of these indicated that they wished to withdraw from membership.

Getting started.—The major activities of the Council are

fully discussed in the chapters following, but the beginnings of the operations are important. The staff, rapidly assembled, found no predetermined program. Its eagerness to achieve tilted the scales in favor of those who wished to do things as against those who wished to take a year to study the situation and then arrive at a program. Moreover, the publicity the organization and its financing had received had produced requests for service. Probably unless the proposed fact finding had been on a self-survey basis, announced at the outset and bringing in the local people as willing participants, no greater progress would have been made by this device than by what was done.

Each staff member began by getting acquainted with the county and its citizens in their own areas of interest. Contacts were often made with the help of the Executive Committee. No invitation to speak was declined. More than 70 organizations were touched in this way in the first year.

From these contacts came an increasing number of persons to the Council offices, in a building put at its disposal by the college, seeking help on programs and other problems of their organizations. This sort of work limited the Council to helping organizations rather than coördinating them, but it gave information as to the aspirations and problems of many groups. Gradually interest groups were brought together to list and work on problems, an important type of fact finding in itself. The first annual report listed 110 *types* of off-campus activities conducted by the 9 white and 2 Negro staff members, many of them such as lectures and attendance at committees repeated many times.

To these somewhat opportunistic activities was added, as the first year wore on, planning on a county-wide basis through committees set up in areas of interest such as health, social welfare, and education.

By the middle of the second year, five major approaches

to community development were clearly defined and were being pursued. These approaches received different emphasis at various times during the remaining years and in the hands of the several staff members, for no attempt was made to standardize their procedures. The rest of the book will illustrate them in detail. They will merely be presented here.

1. *Assistance to organizations and leaders*
   a. Leaders concerned with solving their problems or improving their techniques were given source material, personal advice, and training courses. Committees and organizations were similarly helped in planning or carrying out their activities.
   b. Many organizations operating in the same area were helped to work together by the disinterested leadership of the Council.

2. *Organization of new agencies*
   The best policy the Council found, by and large, was coöperation with existing agencies, persuading them to enlarge their scope to take in untouched areas. But many parts of Greenville County were practically unorganized and needed the stimulation of a new agency such as a council or a dramatic club. There were a few fields such as adult education for the general public in which no agency was equipped to function. Therefore, the organization of a few new agencies was promoted.

3. *Education of college students*
   Practical training in understanding their communities, in recognition of existing problems and techniques of overcoming them, in working with people and in leadership was offered to students of the coöperating college. In-service training to teacher-leaders was also attempted as requested.

4. *Community Councils*
   Community councils were organized because it was found easier for people to think and act in terms of their local com-

munities than in terms of a whole county. Their purposes
were the encouragement of good fellowship and individual
growth, and the solution of community problems.

5. *Social planning and action by interest committees*
People interested in a general area, such as health or government or marketing, were brought together and to work
toward solving common problems.

CHAPTER III

Helping Old Agencies and Starting New Ones

A COMMUNITY'S vitality depends to a large extent upon the vision for service and the efficiency of its various organizations. Leaders and committees determine the policies and procedures of organizations; they should be helped to greater insight and efficiency.

The order in which help was requested by and given to leaders in Greenville County represents steps from simple, obvious demands to more complex and sophisticated requests after a year or two of functioning. First came questions of sources of information or speakers. Then followed suggestions that a staff member sit in on committee planning. Finally some individuals and groups responded to more extended leadership training courses. Eventually the need for new agencies was discovered and the Council helped in organizing these.

The first part of this chapter relates to some of the earlier services of the Council to agencies, organizations, and clubs which were at work when the experiment began. There was nothing unique about most of these. They were of the sort that many professional community organization workers render. Indeed, the more important service activities of the Council staff are recorded in other chapters. Those noted here are simply representative types of assistance by which the staff gained the increasing confidence of the community, things which developed into more fundamental aspects of the program.

HELPING ESTABLISHED AGENCIES

One of the first activities was the assembling of extensive pamphlet files, catalogued under functional heads such as program chairmen would request. This file overlapped very little if at all with the service of the public library, for it stressed simple, brief, readable material in much finer classification than the relatively small public pamphlet collection. It contained no books. It was planned to have this become a part of the public library, but that institution was not equipped to provide sufficient staff service to care for it.

About 4,000 pamphlets were in the file, classified under the headings: Community Activities, Economics, Family, Formal Education, Leisure Time Activities, Religious Activities. Under these were fifty sub-heads. The total cost was approximately $35, a large amount of the material being obtained free.

The pamphlets were never open to indiscriminate general circulation. When individuals or program committees called, they were referred to the file and borrowed liberally. Since Negro library facilities were seriously limited, the Fountain Inn Negro Adult College, described elsewhere, always took a large number. Many other groups borrowed sets for study purposes. College students and the WPA summer school were its chief users. When a WPA assistant was in charge, for two years, the file was in daily use. When, however, there was no one to introduce the wealth of materials to borrowers, the files were used little.

Another way in which information was made available was the preparation of various reference lists, both of materials and of agencies and their services. A few of these were written simply for Negroes and other special groups. The staff gave much incidental assistance in providing information. While they preferred to refer inquirers to sources in order to make them independent of help, there were times when the staff members provided answers. "I've gone as far as I can. Would you mind hunting for a place that prints labels for cans?" asked an agriculture teacher. It took several contacts and a long-distance call to a cannery to provide the answer. Again, a community leader who did not mind approaching local officials with questions did not know how to word a letter to a state officer, and a letter requesting information was sent for him. Each staff member could and did supply answers in the field of his specialty.

From the first requests for program material and techniques local committees sometimes began to meet at the Council Building to discuss possible programs and to survey the available materials.

The most intensive work on the improvement of programs was the conducting of model meetings, when proper techniques and enriched methods were demonstrated. Soon discussions and demonstrations often interrupted the monotony of speakers. One Council staff member was largely responsible for the introduction of panel discussions to Greenville. In fact, with staff members as the original and only advocates for a long time, real group discussion has gradually permeated many organizations.

As emphasis was placed on the importance of trained leadership, groups requested detailed information. The city Parent-Teacher Association was assisted in presenting excellent training institutes for two years. A near-by city asked help for a similar project. A continuing demand for helping local volunteer leaders led to an effective leadership training course which was given in connection with the Citizens Education Center described in another chapter. A men's luncheon club reached an all-time high in the participation and interest of its members when its president consciously applied the principles learned in the course. Many similar instances could be given.

A large amount of staff time was spent throughout the years in working with individual leaders on their problems. Some few came at random to the office, asking how to organize an institute, how to gather together all those interested in children's recreation, what was the minimum parliamentary law for a new president, how to plan a party and lead games. Most leaders were reached on the job, when staff members helped them organize communities, plan committee meetings, or decide how to iron out personality conflicts. These leaders could be helped most when the staff came to them as friends, knowing the names of the dogs and the lists of ailments, listening patiently and pushing only slowly in the direction of better leadership. Some groups had programs well in hand, but wanted help in obtaining more facts about a problem. The studies which were made either for or by them will be described elsewhere.

Finally, leaders and individual agencies were assisted to see problems on which they may not have thought to ask for help. Staff members were responsible for providing leadership in various agencies or areas, and frequently stimulated activity. Certain state members were assigned geographical rather than interest areas. Then it became their business to discover and improve leadership, to help groups work upon their local problems, and to provide the mechanism for a continuing organization. This phase is described in the chapter on local community councils.

This staff specialization grew out of the hectic experiences of the first year when demands were legion and varied talent was limited. Aside from an exhausted staff, the end result was duplication of effort and inadequate techniques. When more specialization was possible, members concentrated and called on one another to assist when groups asked for information outside their area. Thus a staff member could call on the recreation leader to conduct play nights, the county supervisors to work on special teacher problems, or the county librarian to suggest reading lists. Requests for coöperation were soon cleared through the coördinator to the proper staff member.

Probably the most important principle in giving assistance to individuals is that the citizens must know and respect the person whom they approach for help. A newcomer who immediately opens an advice bureau is destined for a fall. The "expert" is accepted best by the groups where he is a member, in which he has demonstrated his worth. Staff members were most effective in their church and civic clubs, or in the areas where they set up committees and had a working acquaintance with many people. Respect also came after speeches, courses, and individual conferences had spread a reputation abroad generally.

A second principle is that help is only accepted when individuals know that they face a problem and want help in solving it. In some areas there is more readiness for group work on problems than in others. In Greenville County educators were keenly aware of several difficulties, recommended a program, and worked on it consistently. On the other hand, health workers recognized no problems that they felt could not be solved individually. That field then shows five years of stalemate or conflict. In another community or at another time it might be the area that was most ready for help.

The best assistance is that which makes individuals and groups increasingly able to resolve their own difficulties. Teaching the problem-solving technique rather than providing an answer, giving a source of information to explore rather than the information, insisting on training in which a new philosophy is acquired, and throwing responsibility for decisions and actions back to the group have all proved to be successful teaching methods.

Starting New Agencies

Prior to the organization of the Greenville County Council for Community Development, the one community-wide coordinating agency was the Community Chest, which followed the usual pattern of agencies of this sort. The accepted agencies such as the Christian Associations, Boy Scouts, several homes for dependent children, a center for Negroes and the like were allotted funds in proportion to their accepted budgetary needs and the amount raised in the annual campaign. These agencies had arisen in response to recognition of particular needs, often stimulated by leaders of national organizations concerned with the promotion of the special interests they represented. There had never been an over-all view of the social needs of city and county. There was no coördination, and overlapping effort was becoming apparent.

Charitable work as such was freely done by the churches, a few clubs, and individuals. The religious tradition of Greenville made the people sensitive to the needs of the poor. Giving to them was viewed as part of their religious duty. People preferred to give "directly" rather than report a case to some agency. As a result the city had become a happy hunting ground not only for resident beggars but also for transients and regular commuters from near-by towns.

Soon after the County Council was organized some of the social workers brought this situation to its attention through a faculty member of the college assigned to the Council staff. Long a resident of the community, favorably known for her leadership in the field, she had the complete trust of these social workers. This underlines the comment made earlier as to the importance of personal relations and of understanding in community organization.

The problem was presented by the staff consultant on social service to an old, conservative club in the city, of which she was a member. It was made up of leading members of the community. Before this group social trends and modern social work were expounded and against that background the local situation was explained. A lively discussion ended in the group asking the County Council to examine the social welfare situation and if necessary present suggestions for improvement. Copies of this action were sent to all the civic and literary clubs in the city.

The Community Council moved with care. Its first step was to call together the citizens interested in and identified with social work. This meeting, which brought an excellent response, resulted in agreement that Greenville needed a Council of Social Agencies, a confidential or social service exchange, a family welfare society or equivalent, and a survey of the existing situation. The Council then constituted this group its social welfare committee. Sub-committees were appointed to explore the problems involved in meeting the recognized needs. The social service consultant of the staff met with all of these committees. The surveys of the local agencies by college students, described in Chapter IV, materially aided the work.

It was decided that a prerequisite to solving the other problems was the organization of a Council of Social Agencies representing the lay and professional leadership of the 29 welfare agencies. Under County Council auspices this was finally decided upon. Constitutions of similar organizations were studied, and an instrument adapted to the local situation was drawn up and agreed to. The qualifications of the officers were carefully evaluated, local leaders compared with the specifications and then interviewed and secured. Permanent committees were set up on family welfare, child welfare, recreation, health, education, and interpretation and publication.

The work of these committees under the guidance of the County Council's consultant and in coöperation with the executives of the agencies proved interesting to the laymen, able for the first time to see the welfare program as a whole. A committee report was brought together in a small pamphlet and printed at the expense of the Chamber of Commerce. Other reports were mimeographed and distributed. The committees also made recommendations to the Council of Social Agencies and the County Council for Community Development, and these two agencies furnished effective means of carrying out many of them.

The Council of Social Agencies has become an accepted part of the community's welfare program. Many laymen have become conscious of welfare needs and techniques. The charity basket of food no longer represents the end and aim of relief. Agency relationships have been improved and overlapping reduced. Some agencies have revamped their programs.

The procedures for effecting the organization of a Family Welfare Society were somewhat similar, though peculiar difficulties had to be overcome. The County Council for Community Development paid the expenses of a staff member of the Family Welfare Association of America to advise with interested local leaders. The methods of similar societies elsewhere were studied with care. The Chest was asked to finance the new agency, and it made a small grant on condition that the agency take over its material relief case work and the case work of another agency. It was impossible on the budget to secure a family work executive, but a local social worker was employed. The City Government furnished office space, clients painted the rooms and local people donated the necessary paint and furniture. As the case load rapidly became impossible the Junior Charities agreed to furnish an additional social worker, and church women were secured and trained as volunteers to help with office work and visiting. Finally, the efforts of two other agencies and that of the Family Welfare Society were completely coördinated, two professionally trained workers employed, and eventually a Negro of comparable training was secured.

Before these developments had gained headway it seemed likely that the records of the Temporary Emergency Relief Administration for the County would have to be transferred to the state capitol with changes in the Federal relief organization. The sub-committee on Confidential Exchange acted quickly and with the aid of private contributions and the Junior Charities secured these records and in coöperation with the social agencies began and now has functioning a confidential exchange which is being used increasingly by the agencies and perhaps equally important, by the churches.

The credit for this last happening goes largely to another coördinating project, the Council of Church Women. In November, 1937, when the Family Welfare Society was finally launched on its career, one of the leading clergymen was made its president. He soon learned of the chaotic condition of private relief in the community and called a meeting of representatives of all the churches in the Greenville metropolitan area. Despite the fact that denominational lines are more tightly drawn in the South than elsewhere over 100 persons attended. The functions of the Family Welfare Society and the Confidential Exchange were explained. It was decided to clear all lists for Christmas giving through these agencies. Later the Council of Church Women was formed. This became the means for securing the volunteer aid for the Family Welfare Society already mentioned. Sub-committees were appointed to work with each church and keep it informed. A beginning has now been made in allocating specific service areas to some of the churches to be cared for regardless of denominational affiliations. The Council contributes over $1,000 a year in non-duplicating material relief. The meetings of the Council of Church Women are devoted to the discussion of some specific welfare problem led by a professional social worker.

In the closing months of the County Council's life the final item in the program laid down at the first was carried through, namely, a survey of the entire social welfare situation. This was a six weeks' study conducted by an outside professional person and sponsored and financed by the Community Chest under a steering committee of laymen.

One other development occurred. It became increasingly clear to the professional and volunteer workers of the Family Welfare Society that many of the disadvantaged families needed legal advice they could not secure. After consultation with every lawyer, the usual series of meetings and study of the situations elsewhere, a Legal Aid Clinic was organized in 1939. The lawyers are giving their services to all cases vouched for by the Family Welfare Society. A different panel of lawyers serves each month. The program and the demands upon it are growing and the lawyers are glad to clear their free work through an authorized agency. The exploitation of the poor is being reduced.

Extended attention has been given to these developments in social welfare because in some respects they are one of the most significant achievements of the County Council for Community Development. True, some and perhaps all of these new agencies would have been formed in time and after trial and error. But the County Council saw very real needs. It proceeded after careful, democratic discussion to facilitate constructive changes in the welfare situation. It had no vested interest in the field and could act without arousing jealousy. It educated the interested and potentially interested constituency at every step. One of the professional consultants brought from outside at one stage was greatly puzzled as to why the terms *Adult Education* and *Social*

Work should be used together. "What have they to do with each other?" she asked. The County Council staff member explained patiently that Adult Education meant, among other things, an understanding of social needs and that such understanding led to social action. Possibly, therefore, the Council has made a contribution at this point outside its county. The Adult Education philosophy of the Greenville County Council for Community Development has nowhere proved more valuable than in the field of social service, and through it ever more people are giving service and being served more intelligently. One evidence of this is the fact that special classes in social work interpretation were requested and offered each year in the Citizens' Education Center, described in Chapter VI, and other classes in group work and "visiting techniques" have been requested and given for both white and Negro church workers, in all cases by Council staff members.

Moreover, the changes are believed to be definite beginnings in social planning in this area. The boards of the several agencies are examining themselves more critically, are seeking better trained workers and are coöperating together more effectively in viewing the community as a whole. This episode in the County Council's history illustrates also its philosophy of not itself assuming permanent responsibilities but rather organizing the community so that needs can be met.

Not all the efforts of the County Council for Community Development were as successful. A County Recreational Council was similarly formed. This Council has arranged for bus service to a state recreation park near Greenville, has conducted fortnightly Saturday afternoon hikes, has made a survey of recreational facilities in and near Greenville, has supported bi-weekly youth parties at an American Legion hut under the auspices of the Y. W. C. A., and has arranged for Red Cross swimming classes in the college gymnasium.

However, a ten weeks' training course conducted with the help of the Council staff for the volunteer workers of four "character building" agencies was not repeated despite good attendance and participation. The plan involved an hour for the whole group on methods and principles, a half hour of recreation demonstration with the teaching of games, and then an hour in which the workers of each agency met separately for applications to their own situations. Difficulty was experienced in getting the complete coöperation from the agency personnel. There was too little participation in planning, and responsibility sharing was not well achieved. Coördination in this area has definitely not been achieved.

Another attempt both to meet a need and effect some coordination failed of consummation, namely the Youth Council. The story of this Council was one of a search for programs. The group wanted to "do something" but was extremely opportunistic. The first activity grew out of an argument as to whether Greenville had enough tennis courts. A list of all available courts was secured but the group lost interest in following through on recreation. A youth survey was enthusiastically proposed. Council staff members led a discussion of means and methods but the project was dropped. A study program was proposed and dropped after the first session when those present decided not to study, but to "do something" about the first problem encountered which had raised a lively discussion. After two meetings they lost interest in that project.

The Youth Council failed for several reasons. The group was heterogeneous in interests and social backgrounds. Many were leaders of church or social groups, with adequate opportunities for expression, with some measure of economic security and little understanding of the problems of other youth less advantaged than they. The group seemed to depend somewhat on adult suggestions but did not feel the need of adult guidance and was desirous of making its own decisions. Possibly a very wise adult leader might have given them a more successful experience in the initial meetings and held them together until they had found themselves. The failure to do this illustrates the precarious balance between democratic self-determination and conducting a successful group by more direct methods.

The County Council did not itself drop work in the youth field, especially in the rural areas of the county as is clear from other chapters. In the last year of the grant, the Council devoted its spring meeting to the youth topic and by using the familiar method of sub-committees began a fairly comprehensive program in this area of interest.

CHAPTER IV

Moving the College Off Its Hill

IT WILL BE REMEMBERED that one of the most important persons in shaping the project known as the Greenville County Council for Community Development and in securing the supporting grant was the president of the local denominational college, B. E. Geer of Furman University. A former college professor, later a business executive, Dr. Geer craved the vitality of experience in actual situations for his students. Out of these two factors the relationship of the Council and the college was born. It was a relationship so intimate and close that it is exceedingly difficult to determine with respect to a number of things in this five-year experiment just which happenings belong in this chapter and which in some of the others.

Originally it had been hoped by the proponents of the project and the foundation that the state university and the state college of agriculture would be able to make some use of the experiment. The former made several faculty members available for consultation in the first years. The latter coöperated throughout in the person of its local extension agents in home economics and agriculture, in the allotment of a generous share of the time of its extension rural sociologist, who unfortunately left the state at the end of two years, and in making available research data concerning Greenville County. But neither state institution made any use of the Council in its own teaching program. Among the hundreds of people who annually visited the Council's office from the second year on were professors and students from most sections of the United States and, indeed, a number of foreign lands but with the few exceptions noted South Carolina was not represented among these pilgrims. The cost of transportation may have been a deterring factor. Time may have been hard to find. Tradition may have had its effect. Even institutional jealousy may have entered in.

But whatever the reasons it was the local college only which utilized the Council and entered deeply into its life. As noted elsewhere it offered a house for the Council headquarters. It utilized the Council staff as teachers and loaned some of its own faculty for staff assignments. Some personnel were paid jointly by the Council and the college.

Preparatory to "getting the college off its hill" certain courses were added to the college offerings such as community organization, community development, southern regional sociology, group leadership, race relations, and recreation leadership. In addition, the courses in introductory and rural sociology were oriented more and more in the direction of field experience. Some excellent field work had been done in a few classes before the Council was formed, especially in the sociology program of the Woman's College of Furman University.

Several courses were added in the education department as well, and the routine practice teaching was given more of a community emphasis. The intent of these courses was to develop community leadership through projects and to increase understanding of community life and social processes. Perhaps the core of this work was in the Group Leadership course, in which seven of the faculty coöperated. Enrollment was limited to upperclassmen who had some leadership relation to a campus organization, scout, youth, religious, or other community groups. These situations offered the practical part of the course content, gave reality to the theory, and permitted a degree of laboratory experience.

One of the devices used for off-campus work was that of field study. Undergraduate students in the departments named have conducted several score of projects of this sort. These were not simply exercises. The careful study of each of the 27 social agencies and charitable institutions, covering purposes, organization, services, methods, financing, constituency and accomplishment was not only appreciated and used by the agencies themselves but also made the basis of a descriptive directory prepared to assist the citizens of city and county to understand the social services available to them and how to secure their help. This study is repeated each year to keep the information up to date. Similarly the city and county welfare setup was studied. A comparable study was made specifically of agencies, federal, state, and local, available to the rural population and a pamphlet prepared.

Spot maps of juvenile delinquency cases and of accidents were made. This last, together with a study of traffic conditions in the city of Greenville, was used by the County Council in persuading the municipal government to make some changes in traffic regulations. Socio-economic surveys of several communities were made which proved most useful in organizing and formulating the programs of area councils in these places. Several pre-ministerial students studied a number of Negro churches. The findings were made available to this group. Nursing service was requested for a deteriorated area on the outskirts of the city. Student nurses were available for the work, but a detailed study of the community was necessary before the program could be started. The sociology students were asked to make the study and did, including a house-to-house survey. On the basis of this information a health center was started and a small community council organized.

As noted in Chapter II, a complete recreational survey was made of Greenville County under an expert loaned to the Council by the Department of the Interior. The sociology students under his supervision collected the sociological data required, including population statistics, recreational facts, and standards of living data. This information was incorporated in the final recreational report.

An ambitious study of Negro housing and economic status was undertaken by one class in coöperation with social science students in the city Negro high school. This is further described in Chapter VI. A fifty-page summary of the findings prepared by the instructor, a member of the Council staff, was given wide publicity in the press, served as the basis for classroom work and many lectures before organizations in the city, and was incorporated as an integral part of a request by the local Housing Authority for funds from the United States Housing Authority. The Federal agency granted the funds but the local share was refused by the City Council. The Greenville County Council for Community Development took an active part in this campaign which missed a successful consummation by a small margin against the sort of opposition that has become well known through the experience of the various Federal housing agencies. Two years later a city referendum overwhelmingly approved the project.

Five hundred high-school students and college freshmen were canvassed by questionnaire and the findings compared with the American Youth Commission's study in Maryland.[1] Another educational study was concerned with pupil retardation and teacher turnover in the rural schools. These studies were undertaken in coöperation with the County Board of Education and the schools. The results were presented at

1. Howard Bell, *Youth Tell Their Story*, American Council on Education, Washington, 1938.

the summer conference of the rural school trustees. This conference is an annual coöperative project of the County Council, the County Board of Education, and the college for the 267 trustees of the county's 89 school districts. A re-check on the part of the study two years later showed some improvement in conditions. The results of this investigation were also summarized for the Council and were influential in some of its educational program.

The other ten studies were more academic yet dealt with real problems such as overlapping bond issues, zoning, sources of revenue in the sheriff's office and the like.

The presence of the County Council staff and the augmenting of the college faculty in the departments of education and sociology in order the better to coöperate in the community development project enabled the college to offer a Master's degree in these two fields. The graduate studies conducted were of similar type and value to the Council. They dealt with some of the communities in the county, with topical studies of aspects of community life such as recreation, rural youth, textile mill employees' families, the cost of education in South Carolina colleges, the Holiness Movement in Greenville County, and so on through a list of about 20 studies. A number of these were mimeographed, used in the communities concerned, and helped in the organization of local councils. Some were discussed before county and state teachers' associations and ministerial groups. Several will be mentioned later in other connections.

There is, of course, nothing unusual in the type of surveys and service research here described. They are familiar tools, especially in graduate work and among social and educational agencies. The uniqueness of the situation described lay in the fact that the work done not only related to real, often pressing needs and problems, but also became immediately usable in action programs because of the coöperative relationship existing between the County Council and the college. The surveys did not lie forgotten in the files of a professor. They passed into community circulation.

There were several outcomes of this situation that need cognizance in evaluating the success of the effort "to get the college off its hill." Graduates taking up positions began to use what they had learned in this experience in their own jobs and communities. Even students in their summer vacations, if not working, began to assist home organizations in some of the ways employed at Greenville. Many became quite interested in the socio-economic aspects of life in their home communities and some helped organize or became officers in youth clubs, credit unions, recreational programs, drama groups and the like. Others worked in the County Agent's offices and the Campbell Folk School, and took part in summer recreational activities of the Scouts, the Y. M. C. A. or Y. W. C. A., the city and near-by state parks. Students of the college helped to elect a former classmate to the state legislature and after his election were in no sense backward in telling him what they expected him to do.

Student interest and faculty desire alike combined in carrying them into other situations. Groups attended meetings of local community councils and of the County Council, the Municipal Council, the Community Chest, and various welfare agencies. They also attended and, at first to the disquietude of some, participated in the State Conferences of Social Work and a regional conference on Marriage and Family Life. The first-named organization now has a youth section on whose program some of these students have appeared more than once. When the Council and the Agricultural Extension Service put on a series of discussion meetings in 1938 on the cotton situation, students after participating with others in the training, served as discussion leaders in ten of the fifty-five groups.

Field trips were part of the plan, and various classes attended sessions of the state legislature, the county court, the county Democratic convention, and the city council, and visited cotton mills, labor unions, hospitals, schools, and welfare institutions. As a result it was easy to secure officers of these and other agencies to come to the hill and participate in class discussions. Various representatives of ten types of institutions have coöperated in this way, many of them every year. Visits were also made to meetings of local community councils and various rural enterprises.

One incident is typical of the way students influenced by this program have sought to carry through. After studying in classroom and on the field the work of the State Welfare Department, a class in public welfare decided it was a pity that high-school pupils and laymen did not understand better the whole program of this agency. They also determined that the moving picture was the best medium of instruction. They enlisted the coöperation of the public officials and produced films on the penal system, the health program, and on the total work of the Department of Public Welfare and its institutions. These have been shown to teachers' conventions and to schools, colleges, and lay groups. Radio has also been employed in some projects.

What has been true of students has obviously held for the faculty as well. Council staff members in the very nature of their jobs were out in the field more than in the classroom but others who have coöperated with the Council have also carried a load of lectures, local and state board memberships, Council committee memberships, teaching adult education classes, consultation with and membership in local organizations. There is, of course, no study of the faculties of denominational colleges to show how much of this sort of community, as contrasted with church and denominational, work they do. It is safe to say that few could show such a record as that which stands to the credit of the Furman faculty over these last years. The relationships of the faculty with community organizations and their knowledge of the Council frequently resulted in joint projects or in the quick and understanding support of some plan initiated either by some agency or the Council by all the others. Coördination was thus on a functional basis both by organization action and by personal relationships. Both are necessary. Moreover, the college encouraged the faculty to so serve, and in the case of those who became staff members of the Council it lightened the teaching loads somewhat to make their community service the more possible and effective.

The deans of both the men's and women's campuses of the college have testified to the value of the relationship of the Council and the College and to the value to the college of closer contact with the ongoing life of the community. Dean R. N. Daniel has remarked, "It makes possible education in which there is marriage of thought and action. And the thing to be noted especially is that the action is constructive in character."

Dean Virginia Thomas is equally enthusiastic. She points out that for a decade women students elected to the leadership of campus activities had held a week-end retreat to discuss problems of leadership but that this discussion showed the lack of concrete experiences. For the last five years the discussions have been "entirely different." As one student put it, "I wonder what has been discussed at camp in the years when there was no Greenville County Council for Community Development?"

Students who have had contact with the program are enthusiastic. "It has made education purposive," and "It has taught me how ideals become realities," are two representative comments. Students with this experience readily find jobs in social agencies or show effective leadership.

The ways in which one particular student related his four years of study at Furman to the Council program is enlightening as an example. A resident of a rural community in the county, he assisted in the Negro housing study, made a socio-economic survey and map of his community which served as a basis for planning, became an officer in his community's newly organized credit union and youth club, participated in a youth survey, served as supply pastor in rural churches, and spoke before a civic club in behalf of the community chest. Most of these activities were part of his course work in college.

In the summer of 1939 members of the Council joined with the authorities of the college to provide a demonstration school intended primarily to help county teachers. A rural school near Greenville was used. Here a curriculum including observation, discussion of observed practice, instruction and practice in arts and crafts, writing of pre-plans, and philosophy of education was offered. This effort is another indication that the college realized an obligation to the teachers in its area.

Another interesting project was initiated last year by the education and sociology departments. Prospective practice teachers spend the two weeks in September previous to the opening of the college (the public schools have usually opened the first week in September) in studying the community and the school either in their home community or some community in which they have relatives or friends. A manual for this study has been developed coöperatively by the students and teachers. This program fits into two courses of the professional program, Educational Sociology and School Organization and Administration.

The demonstration school was continued in the summer of 1940 and a new venture, a workshop for high-school teachers, undertaken. The workshop, held on the campus, was sponsored and supported by the Commission on Teacher Education of the American Council on Education and the school systems of Greenville, Parker District, and the county.

In the summer of 1941 the Southeastern Workshop in Community Development was added to the summer school program with the assistance of the General Education Board. This project brought together more than fifty outstanding people from the southeastern states to study and evaluate the work of the Greenville County Council for Community Development and to discuss how its conclusions can be applied in their local situations. Many of the enrollees were persons sent by the General Education Board.

Some time before the workshop was set up the schools of the city and county, in coöperation with the Greenville County Council for Community Development and the college, became one of thirty-four units coöperating with the Commission on Teacher Education of the American Council on Education. This selection was made because of the program described in this chapter and indeed this whole report. The education committee of the Greenville County Council for Community Development became the coördinating agency for the city and county schools. The committee is now sponsoring a large number of projects looking toward the improvement of pre-service and in-service training of teachers.

Another educational effort with sociological analysis through field course procedure as its objective is at least in part a result of the activities of the County Council. Columbia University and the Open Road since 1939 have united in a field course in southern conditions and chose Greenville County for its locale because of the Council. The head of the Department of Sociology of the local college was used as leader. A small group of graduate students studied agriculture, labor, health, education, and race relations in the county at first hand. Beyond the necessary background each specialized in his own area of professional interest. Among the most interesting results have been changes in point of view of both Southerners and Northerners indicative of new knowledge and understanding.

The discussion just above would seem to indicate that on any basis of evaluation the program described has justified itself. It is not to be supposed, however, that it has been uniformly successful. Some of the problems with reference to staff and faculty were noted in Chapter II. Not all the studies made had practical outcomes. Nor were all the departments of the college affected. Education and sociology contributed and profited most. To a lesser degree this was true of economics, dramatics, home economics, political science and religion. But some departments of the college were openly critical both of the Council as such and its relationship to the campus. Others preferred to wait and see what results the experiment would produce. Thus only students in the interested departments were exposed to the program. Some were bewildered by the differences in methods and procedure between the traditional classroom teaching and those in the departments engaged in this program. There was difficulty in arranging transportation to rural projects. Financing such field work was a real problem. Adjusting class meetings to meet community demands was a problem for both faculty and students. Vacations, too, often disorganized students' community relationships. But the enthusiasm of faculty and of almost all students participating and the results accomplished would seem to warrant further experimentation over wide areas to discover techniques for enlarging student and faculty participation in rebuilding community life.

CHAPTER V

Community Councils

VERY EARLY in the history of the Greenville County Council for Community Development it became evident that few people could think and plan in terms of the entire county. The very diversity of the county was one effective barrier to such an enterprise. The experience of the sharecropper in the southern tier of townships had little save poverty in common with that of the mountain whites in the north. The textile mill operator lived a daily life quite different from either of these. The cultured and often prosperous leaders of the county seat city were fully occupied with the problems and interests immediately around them. The occupational differences between trade, manufacturing, and agriculture, the leading ways of making a living, resulted in natural barriers to complete understanding. Only in education, and to a less extent social welfare and agriculture, where there was qualified professional leadership, was planning and action on a county basis conspicuously successful. In part, this was due to the fact that the solutions of some of the recognized problems lay in areas larger than the county itself. State or regional influences were determinative or even as in the case of cotton, national and international. In part, also, the reason for this lay in lack of practice, even lack of opportunity in working together.

In time the County Council for Community Development might have overcome this difficulty; in fact it measurably did. But the Council early decided that in order to bring its service to the entire county, in order to increase the amount of thinking and planning together, it would be well to experiment with the idea of organizing local community councils on a school district basis. It was felt that this step would also make possible an attack on some of the county's diverse problems in the communities where the people lived and thus strengthen the whole enterprise.

In all, eight of these councils were organized, five in the open country, one in a rural suburban neighborhood, one in a medium-sized village, one in a town. These eight places were in three of the county's four regions, only the mountainous north being unrepresented. Various factors entered into the choice of these eight among the twice as many recognized communities of the county. One was the desire of the staff to experiment with a variety of situations, another was the interest and ability of the local leaders. Two of the eight were organized largely as a result of County Council stimulation. In another, the school and a County Council staff member were the prime movers. In two the professional leaders in the school were primarily responsible. In another the school and a woman's club initiated the area council. The P.T.A. was the primary mover in a seventh case and the final one came from a variety of stimuli. The outcome of these area councils varied from almost complete failure to exceptional success. All in all they present an instructive chapter in the County Council's history.

The most successful council was in a somewhat unique, wholly rural community, the integrating factor of which was the high school. The area was unusual in a number of particulars. It had no trade center, no telephones, almost no tenant-operated farms and only four Negro families in a population of over 3,000.

The area council here was a natural growth. The newly elected superintendent of schools probably had no idea of helping to organize an area council when he first approached the County Council for help in improving his high school and its six feeder schools at the suggestion of an educator who was also prominent in the Council. A conference of several hours each week between the teachers of the high school area and a Council staff member followed. As a by-product the teachers organized a dramatic group and produced several plays under the direction of a member of the college's drama department which frequently coöperated with the Council. Other interests began to be expressed and soon people in the area were wondering about a community council.

At this point two Council staff members, the superintendent of schools and a school trustee, conferred and canvassed the problems of the community which the people might solve themselves. Next a meeting was called of all the school trustees, the ministers and the teachers. This group listed ten problems and requested an organization to meet them.

The Council staff members persuaded them, however, to take an intermediate step. Meetings were held in each of the seven school districts to discuss the plan, to list problems and if desired to elect representatives to an area council should one be formed. This procedure resulted in the organization of an area council in which schools, churches, home demonstration clubs and youth were represented. It was the county's first community council.

It should be noted that the process leading up to these organizations was more democratic than that employed in launching the County Council itself. The professional leaders in the community were held back until the people in every school district had been given an opportunity to discuss and register their opinion. This educational procedure took more time, it was costly in terms of county council staff coöperation, but it was effective. Any other method among an independent farm-owner group such as the one in this community, would have worked under self-imposed handicaps and might have failed.

The first problems listed have largely been solved. Recreation for young and old has been improved. The drama club for instance, now includes a considerable number of adults in addition to teachers. It has played before audiences in the county, and in Atlanta before one southern region conference. Children, youth, and adults are enjoying a softball league in season. The schools have been improved. Some of the achievements in this community may be summarized as follows:

1. A coöperative store was organized in July, 1938, with 12 members. At first it did little more than pool orders for feed, fertilizer, and spray materials. In January, 1940, the coöperative bought out a crossroads store and filling station which had a business of less than $500 a month. In the balance of the year the store sales exceeded $13,000; fertilizer, etc., topped $3,000, a total of over $16,000. To the summer of 1941 business was running at the rate of $20,000 a year. There are now 78 members who received a 2 per cent patronage dividend in January, 1941.

2. There is also a Community Potato Curing House owned by the high school but managed by the Coöperative. Money for materials was secured on a note signed by 20 men, most of them members of the Coöperative. Construction was done by the WPA. The house is open to the entire community. The capacity is 5,000 bushels. In 1940 110 families stored 2,100 bushels at a charge of from 10c to 12½c per bushel depending on the quantity. In 1941 the house was used practically to capacity.

3. A community cannery is operated jointly by the high school and the Coöperative. In 1940 approximately 16,000 cans of vegetables, fruit, and meat were put up by 164 fam-

ilies. Patrons do their own work, merely paying for cans and service at the rate of 5c a quart can.

4. Starting in April, 1939, 39 persons formed a federally chartered credit union which by May, 1941, had nearly $1,000 in paid-up share capital and had loaned all told nearly $2,500. All loans have been repaid on time.

5. A community egg hatchery is operating.

6. The community idea has also been carried over into plant beds for sweet potatoes, tomatoes, peppers, and a few other vegetables.

7. A beautification program has been carried on beginning with the grade school and church grounds but including finally many homes.

8. A modest but adequate clinic building was coöperatively built and the County Council nurse provided with adequate supplies and equipment. The program reached all schools. When the special funds on which the nurse was employed expired the community raised funds for a continuance of the extensive health program for some time.

9. A branch of the County library has been secured and housed in quarters provided.

10. Hot lunches are now provided in all feeder schools and in the high school.

11. The Area school faculty had an important part in initiating a collective buying program for schools in the county as well as the development of a County Teachers Materials Bureau and Coöperative Store. They also initiated a publication known as the Greenville County Teachers Newsletter, which is circulated among the teachers of Greenville County.

12. Progress was made in the development of coöperation between feeder schools and high school toward the community centered school program.

13. There was also great improvement in the achievement records in the schools, especially in reading.

14. Development of a coöperative attitude among the area people which has extended out into other communities near and far. Many carloads of people in this area have gone to other communities to aid them in initiating and implementing a community improvement program.

This improvement in the schools is, of course, not an achievement solely of the local council or even the parent county body. But it came because a Council staff member worked with the teachers at their request; because the school trustees approved the progress they saw and were kept in touch with the larger aspects of the educational situation, through the annual institute for school trustees or directors described in Chapter IV; because the parents recognized not only the improvement in their children but also were aware of direct services to themselves as adults and hence supported the school more loyally; because the area council was making the community a better place, which reacted on the school and its pupils; and because the schoolteachers and officials began to see that the school was in and a part of, not separate from, the community.

The coöperative projects could perhaps have come to pass without the Council but it was the County Council that helped send the agricultural teacher, with nearly a dozen others from the County, to study the coöperative movement in the Antigonish Country of Nova Scotia and it was the area council which gave him immediate access to the community when he desired to promote the coöperative idea. It was also the habit of successful coöperation through the Council in achieving other things which made the community ready later on to tackle these rather considerable enterprises. Naturally, also, this community has been highly successful in its annual live-at-home program, described in Chapter VI, and in other activities.

A somewhat similar community in the same region of the county organized in much the same manner as the one just described, but was not quite as successful. It listed as its most important problems for which it immediately sought answers, the securing of rural electrification for all eight of its neighborhood school districts and a drainage project involving several creeks in the community. Both these projects involved dealing with state or federal agencies on electrification, or with the dominant public utility of the area. They were, therefore, far more difficult than those selected by the community described above. The people worked hard. The utility representatives, for instance, were presented with a map showing every road, every home, and an indication of what light and power equipment each householder would install. The utility objected, however, to servicing some of the less densely populated parts of the area. The local people wanted current on an "all or none basis." They were near no federal project and did not have a sufficient volume of business to make the erection of a coöperative plant feasible, especially since the utility already reached into the edge of the territory.

Neither of the projects, after three years of work, and despite help from the County Council, has been consummated. The Council therefore was somewhat discouraged. Its projects were too ambitious for first steps and against that failure the other considerable achievements seem less fruitful than they really are. These include the securing of a community school in one neighborhood, health work in four, a youth program in three, a local citizens' education center (see Chapter VI), very successful outdoor play nights (including the securing of floodlight equipment) during the summer months, a good participation in the live-at-home campaign, and the conduct of a successful coöperative store.

Another difficulty in this community lay in the selection of the first president. He was unable to delegate responsibility, and eventually and naturally the people allowed him to do what was done. The school had a new superintendent who was little interested in anything outside the school. The experience of the County Council demonstrates that in this sort of program the interested coöperation and preferably the actual leadership in some capacity, of the professional representative of the school and if possible of the leading churches, is almost a *sine qua non* of success.

The success attained by this Council in all but its two ambitious projects came in part because of an interesting variation in organizational procedure. Most of its eight neighborhoods had local councils and four of these especially did effective work in meeting neighborhood problems and serving neighborhood interests.

Even some degree of initial achievement will not save a local community council from eventual failure. The Council formed in a town of 3,000 people illustrates this. The superintendent of schools and the president of an important club were active in the County Council and after three meetings in their own community organized an area council with committees to study and programize on health, recreation, education, social welfare, economic improvement and racial problems. The social welfare committee, with help from some of the executives of agencies in the county seat city and from the County Council set up a confidential exchange and in other ways improved the handling of relief in the community. A Citizens' Educational Center was successfully conducted, judged by enrollment and attendance, but not repeated. Similarly a school for Negroes offering practical courses in child care, health, home gardening, and several other subjects was conducted and well supported by this group. Again this was not repeated. A Little Theatre was organized and after a successful experience, following usual Council procedure, it organized separately and has continued. Other plans were suggested, studied, and dropped. The Council has not met as a whole for about two years.

Several factors account for this situation. A president was chosen who did not have time to give to the enterprise because of very arduous duties in his job. The staff member assigned by the County Council as the consultant for this area council did not give continued leadership after the organization seemed well launched. Some of the most important officers or sponsors were not on good working terms. There were some sharp cleavages in the community and some basic conflicts that were not adequately recognized at the start. As a result, some of those interested feared to coöperate lest they offend important people who were tacitly or actually opposed to the project. It is more than likely that most if not all of these handicaps could have been overcome by more careful and continuing leadership from the County Council staff member, especially if there had been enough advance study of the situation to discover the pitfalls. In a community of this size it is especially important in community organization to know the situation thoroughly and not be lulled into over-confidence because the auspices seem adequate and the proponents enthusiastic.

The experience in the medium-sized village, the center of a considerable tributary trade and school area, was more fortunate. This community was organized by the Council itself. Before the organization, however, there had been a survey by two local school men as part of their work for graduate degrees at the college. In this survey teachers, school children, and citizen committees had coöperated and the results were made available to them. These results were considered by a group of citizens who decided to do something about the problems uncovered. The area council resulted.

Among its projects have been a clean-up campaign, which resulted in clearing up literally scores of unsightly spots and which even razed three abandoned and decaying buildings; the improvement and beautification of school grounds and of many homes; the securing of a full-time public health nurse; the conducting of an area-wide health program, the holding of a yearly flower show, the construction of a community park; sponsoring of a very successful summer recreation program for adults; successful annual coöperation in the live-at-home campaign; and possibly most important the erection and equipping of an adequate three-room brick public library. This last was made possible by a WPA grant secured by the County Council, but the citizens oversubscribed the town's share of the cost. This was a direct result of the survey.

This Council is the most informal of all those organized. It has no membership list and no standing committees. For each new task the president gathers together those most interested. There is an element of freshness and interest in each such new group. The choice is limited, however, by the acquaintanceship of the president, and the open country areas of the community are not proportionately represented. The participation has never been as wide as in some of the other councils.

Another area council similarly initiated, in addition to carrying through most of the activities described above, was one of those to organize a successful federal Credit Union, purchased a movie projector and secured a doctor on a coöperative plan, and boasts of having had ten of its fourteen teachers at summer school in 1940. In many respects it was fully as successful as the first case described.

A detailed account of the organization, successes, and failures of the other area councils would not add very much to an understanding of the process beyond what has already been written. One of these had elements of peculiar difficulty, a three-school district community which asked help through a Mothers' Club of one of the schools. Organization here was initially on a school district basis, and only after the three neighborhood clubs discovered common problems was a community council launched. The immediate effort to organize on a community basis would have failed. The area was partly rural, partly suburban. Many of its people were newcomers. It had no traditions and few, if any, ties beyond those of parents to the schools their children attended.

Another not too successful local council in a rural area without telephones did, however, evolve a scheme of mapping the community with every home and the names of its inmates recorded. On the basis of this one family was made responsible for reaching five others until a complete coverage of the area was effected. This device was quite important when new projects needing a complete coverage of all homes were undertaken and overcame to some degree the lack of telephonic communication.

The most surprising failure occurred where it was least expected. The high school of this community had long been, especially through its vocational agricultural department, a center of community services. Through it, a number of things had already been accomplished which in other places the Councils worked hard to achieve, such as a sweet potato curing house, a shop open to residents for repairing or building farm and home equipment, a community cannery, seed-treating equipment, a picnic grove, a community house, and a coöperative which managed a number of these enterprises. It developed, however, that almost the sole emphasis in this program had been economic. The things had been done *by* the school *for* the people. No leadership had been developed. Indeed, the school itself was not very democratically conducted and had a very large teacher turnover. No effort had been made to heal serious antagonisms in the community. There was also a large and shifting tenant population. These were handicaps the County Council could not overcome despite some successful health and recreation work.

Except for the Negro Council, described in Chapter VII, not one of these community councils was in the metropolitan area of Greenville. There were a number of reasons for this. There are few natural communities in cities that possess enough common interests or other integrating factors to foster community spirit. Leadership in a city the size of Greenville is city-wide; neighborhood problems are not recognized.

In the textile section outside the municipality but within the metropolitan area, the natural boundaries were set by the employees residing, as is usual in the South, near their various mills. This section, known from its school organization as the Parker District, had had for years a sanely progressive and effective school system which had attracted much attention from without and considerable confidence within. Even before the County Council was organized its adult education program, known as the People's College, had been functioning, though this last effort was aided by the Council. Through this program 15 "mill village" councils had already been set up, devoted primarily to home improvement and beautification.

The Council regarded this as furnishing the basis for greatly expanded programs, but with so much of the county unorganized it turned its first attention to outside the metropolitan area. The problem of adequate democratic organization within the city was recognized and the Council at one time considered an experiment in this field, but limitations of staff prevented carrying out this purpose.

It is apparent from these narratives that the type of people, quality of local leadership, and the degree both of local institutional support and of County Council assistance were factors in the success of the area councils. Adequate and continuous educational work was clearly essential. The programs were flexible and varied and fitted to local conditions, but a number of activities were common to several or most of the local councils. The communities with these councils were also more informed about and more coöperative with the County Council. Failures came from poor leadership and in general inadequacies that were the reverse of the qualities and assets present in the successful communities.

The use of the word failure, however, is chiefly adequate and fair only with reference to specific projects that were or were not consummated. But there is a larger and possibly more important consideration than this. Local leadership was improved by contact with the County Council program. There is more awareness of problems, more willingness to face rather than dodge issues, more reliance in community coöperation as a worthwhile method. These things are not measurable but they are noted by those who know and work in even communities whose councils were not as successful as those described. In the long run this may be the most important contribution of the County Council, one that will outlast any other.

CHAPTER VI

Social Planning by Committees

THE FOREGOING chapters have described important units of the work of the five-year experiment in community organization by the Greenville County Council for Community Development. One more such unit, that dealing with the Negro part of the program, remains to be described. But first attention must be given to various activities in special areas of interest. Some of these were in charge of committees. Some were initiated by the Council, usually through staff members. They concern such things as adult education, special service to rural areas, health, and activities in the areas of economics and government.

It should be emphasized that the Council had other areas of interest, in some of which more satisfying progress was made than in those to be discussed in this chapter. But a number of such have been described in connection with other chapters. Recreation, for instance, was a part of the program of every local council. The summer play nights, soft ball leagues, drama guilds, youth clubs and other activities made a continuous and successful appeal. The recreational consultant of the Council, furnished by the WPA, was in constant demand. A chapter report could have been made of this program. But in the case of recreation, as with several other areas, the work was done almost exclusively through or under the auspices of local organizations. It was the philosophy of the Council that this should be done wherever possible and equally wherever possible this report has been made in the same way.

SPECIAL SERVICE TO RURAL AREAS

The County Council gave perhaps a disproportionate share of its energy, especially in the last three years to the rural part of the county. In part this was because the greater need seemed to be there. In contrast to the city, which like most was over-organized, the rural part of the county, like much of the rural South, was definitely under-organized. In part, the attention to the rural areas was due to the fact that projects started within the city could be handed over to permanent sponsoring organizations once they were safely under way. This has been particularly well illustrated in the account of the social welfare developments in Chapter III.

The local community councils described in Chapter V were with two exceptions rural, and one of these was rural-suburban. The youth clubs, community nights, and recreational counseling for rural schoolteachers also were largely rural. The educational work gave much attention to the rural schools. In addition there were several projects which deserve special attention. The first of these was the Cotton Discussion Program.

Cotton Discussion Program.—In the fall of 1937, fifteen months after the Council started, South Carolina farmers were concerned over the price of cotton. Some of them interpreted "parity" as restoration of World War One price peaks. All of them were disappointed by the existing price level. There was little understanding of the national and international forces that were depressing the prices of all export crops. The Agricultural Adjustment Administration had established shortly before a Program Study and Discussion Section in an effort to give farm people a clearer grasp of the social and economic problems confronting them. An experiment in an intensive discussion program was attempted in Greenville County with the Council coöperating with the Discussion Specialist of the AAA for the southeastern states.

Simple materials, charts, graphs, and discussion outlines were prepared with special reference to the place of the state and county in the cotton situation. Fifty-five simultaneous groups to discuss the cotton problem were arranged to meet in as many schoolhouses on three evenings in one week. Discussion leaders were secured from farm men and women, County Council staff members, agricultural leaders, local college faculty and students, and rural schoolteachers. A series of training conferences were held for these leaders, a number of whom had never participated in this sort of enterprise before. Despite some very cold weather the series was carried through. While a few scheduled meetings attracted no attendants the maximum was 110 and the average 22, so that 1,100 cotton farmers participated in the project. Many of the groups brought in from 6 to 12 suggestions as to "ways out," and most of these put high on the list the proposal that the South should raise all the foodstuffs possible— the Live-at-Home program.

Live-at-Home Program.—For several years the Agricultural Extension Service (Smith-Lever) and the Vocational Agricultural and Home Economics Teachers (Smith-Hughes) had advocated such a program, especially in the South for farm families. Briefly this meant that first consideration in the farm plan would be given to growing all the food necessary to feed both the family and the stock. This idea is particularly applicable in the South where climatic conditions make possible the raising of everything necessary for a balanced diet with the exception of coffee and sugar.

While this program had been stressed, the pressure of tradition, the custom of growing all cotton and purchasing supplies at the store for "cash" still prevailed. The government crop control program released many acres from cotton production, but these "idle" acres found their way grudgingly into gardens for the family, or feed for the stock.

It was at this juncture that the Farm Income Committee of the County Council's program conceived the plan of bringing social approval to bear on the Live-at-Home idea. The interest of the Governor was secured. He readily agreed not only to sign a Certificate of Recognition for every farm family that reached a goal of 75 per cent of the complete standard for living at home, but accepted the invitation to come to Greenville County in November, 1939, and present the certificates in person.

It was May, 1939, before the committee conceived the idea. This was too late to set up machinery to cover the county in an enrollment campaign. But through the Home Demonstration Clubs, through the Farm Security Administration Home Economics Supervisor, and through a few vocational agriculture teachers, 227 families "signed up," and 184 white and Negro families were awarded certificates by the Governor, signed by him and also by the State Director of Agricultural Extension, by the State Director of Vocational Education, and by the Chairman of the Greenville County Live-at-Home Committee. The certificates for white families were awarded in connection with the Fall County Council Meeting at a rural high school, twenty-five miles from the city attended by over 500 farm and city people. The Governor challenged the committee to enroll 1,000 families in the second year's effort.

· The campaign got under way at once. On the final date 1,002 families had signed to participate in the 1940 program.

In 1941, 2,000 signed up, 25 per cent of all the farm homes in the county. Despite terrible weather all but one of the communities of the county was represented at the final round-up luncheon.

These results were not achieved without considerable

effort. Captains and teams had to be secured in every community. The Council office had to keep a check on every center. In the final weeks of the campaign daily post card bulletins and reminders were mailed.

Other agencies coöperated. The State Agricultural College mailed to each enrollee a monthly Garden Letter giving suggestions for planting and for the best garden practice for that month. The Home Demonstration agents included better gardening in their club programs. Canning and pressure cooker demonstrations have been repeatedly given. Seven of the rural high schools have "canneries," fully equipped, usually operated by the community coöperative under the supervision of the vocational agricultural teacher. Guidance is given in preparing fruits, vegetables, and meats for canning and a small fee covers the cost of cans and upkeep of the equipment. In addition to this practical service some of the vocational agriculture and home economics teachers hold evening classes when better gardening is taught.

The County Live-at-Home Committee is composed of the Chairman of the Council's Farm Income Committee, the Chairman of the Council of Farm Women, the Chairman of the County Agricultural Committee, a leading farmer and a farm woman chosen by the vocational agriculture teachers, the County Agent, the Home Demonstration Agent, a vocational agriculture teacher and a home economics teacher.

The idea has spread all over the state and into several adjoining states.

More than any other activity of the Council the Live-at-Home program reached into every community. Leaders had to be found and enlisted even where there were no local councils. This, plus the excellent newspaper and local radio publicity brought to the whole county some knowledge of the fact that there was such an organization as a County Council. The attention the enterprise attracted developed some pride in the people of the county, and healthy pride in home community and county is an asset in community organization. It was notable but natural that the proportions of homes signed up and of accomplishment were higher in those places which had local councils than in the others. Less staff effort was also required in such places. This is just another indication that in a county development of the type attempted in Greenville County local community organizations, affiliated with the county body, greatly facilitate the working out of the program.

Farm income.—The Live-at-Home program clearly raised the standard of living for the participants but the agricultural leaders and the County Council realized that the problem of raising farm income in the county was far larger than this. As noted in Chapter I the county is one of small farms, even in Southern terms, and the cotton growers perforce produced at a higher cost than that obtaining in the southwestern states. Everyone seemed to agree that one or more substitutes must be found for cotton but there was little or no agreement on what should be substituted. The Council decided that perhaps there was enough intelligence in the county at least to explore the problem and perhaps initiate some experiments. It called an Economic Conference made up of the agricultural leaders of the county, 12 farmers, 12 merchants selected by the Chamber of Commerce, and 12 consumers not connected with farming or trade.

Sixty people attended this meeting which was carefully prepared for. After a thorough discussion of several hours a continuation committee of 15 was appointed which met fortnightly for some months. Five possible substitutes for cotton were thoroughly studied. It was decided to begin with poultry since 90 per cent of the eggs and 80 per cent of the poultry used in Greenville County came from outside the state.[1] With the coöperation of the Chamber of Commerce, the State College of Agriculture, and the County Council, a number of meetings were held to explore various angles of the problem and finally there was a two-day poultry conference. Though the attendance was somewhat smaller than expected the net results were an increased interest in poultry for home use and market. In two communities many new commercial flocks were started. In one a poultry coöperative was organized. The Chamber of Commerce ran large advertisements announcing "broilers" from these communities.

It became increasingly apparent that marketing was the bottleneck of the problem of disposing of more home-grown food. Local city merchants must have a continuous and dependable supply of goods of dependable quality. Farmers need to market their perishable crops when they are ready, but merchants have no knowledge of when this will be. The Council's Committee felt that a marketing expert would be a good investment. The Extension Service of the State College of Agriculture, the county agricultural agent, the State Director of Vocational Agriculture, and the Chamber of Commerce all approved the idea. It is expected that such a person can be employed. The need is made clear by a typical experience.

A farmer in Greenville County grew a large quantity of butter beans. When ripe he and his wife stayed up all night shelling them. They had a bushel of shelled butter beans, a sizeable quantity. Early the next morning he started for the city to sell his beans. The stores would have gladly

1. Disregarding truck shipments the annual rail import into Greenville was over 316,000 bushels of 8 commodities, over 30,000 tons of 3 others, a million pounds of lard and lard substitute, over 20,000 head of cattle and hogs, over 115,000 pounds of butter, and 70 boxcar loads of peanuts. The live-at-home program clearly had an urban side.

taken Greenville County beans, but they had already contracted for their supply from produce men. He spent the entire day peddling them from door to door with no success. Returning home at night tired out and disgusted he put them in the refrigerator determined to can them at the community cannery the next day. When he reached the cannery they were moulded and had to be thrown out.

Greenville County alone could go far to remedy this situation. With a county inventory of dates, quantity, and quality of production from various farms a marketing specialist could deliver a steady supply to markets which he had previously contacted. In coöperation with agriculture teachers and county agents he could teach farmers how to package. In case of the beans, the Greenville County Marketing Agent would have known that farmer X was to have a bushel of shelled butter beans on a certain date. He would have arranged with the vocational agriculture teacher in farmer X's area to show him how to package the shelled beans in quart boxes covered with cellophane, perhaps with the farmer's name on a label inside. The agent would then have contracted with various stores to take these beans on the day they were to be marketed.

Citizens Education Center.—The next special project of the County Council to be discussed originally concerned only the city.

As the Council program went into its third year, the feeling grew among several of the staff members that there was need for more general adult education work in the community. This need had been manifested in several phases of the program and was found to be included in the objectives of several of the Council committees, notably the Education Committee and the Committee on Economics and Government. The idea came that a number of efforts in this field might be concentrated in one large program or education center.

Realizing that the men's luncheon clubs of the city are often important in putting ideas across, it was decided that they should be approached with the idea. A meeting of the chairmen of the education committees of the four luncheon clubs was called and the idea of a coördinated and enlarged adult educational program was put before them. This group endorsed the plan and in turn presented it to the Interclub Council which approved and passed it on to the Executive Committees of the individual clubs.

All four clubs agreed to sponsor the project, each appointed three members to the Board of Directors of the education center, with the County Council appointing an additional three members. In December, 1940, two other civic clubs were added to the sponsoring group.

A staff member of the Council served as secretary. Committees were appointed on publicity, courses and faculty, building arrangements, finance, assembly period. The following schedule was decided upon: 7:00-7:30, assembly period; 7:40-8:30, first period; 8:40-9:30, second period. The name Citizens Education Center was adopted for the project. It was decided that there should be six Monday night meetings.

Estimates of probable enrollment ranged from 100 to an optimistic 600 but by the time the first session was ended 1,400 had registered, most of them for two courses. A 25c registration fee per course covered the incidental expenses. The new Senior High School Building was used. The faculty, who were about equally divided between the local college professors, high-school teachers and competent townspeople served without pay. The 33 course titles follow: Household Management, How to Be Happily Married,

How to Feed the Family Correctly, How to Listen to Music, Recent Books and Plays, Making Friends With the Stars, History of Greenville, How to Lead Groups, Handicrafts for Everyone, Your Health and How to Keep It, Your Money's Worth in Food and Drugs, Reasonable Aids to Personal Beauty, Photography for All, How to Speak in Public, How to Rear Our Children—Pre-Adolescent, The New Fashions and You, Personality Problems in Everyday Life, Everyday English, Keeping Up with Science, How to Rear Our Children—Adolescent, Highlights in International Affairs, Taxation and Government Finance, Flowers the Year Round, Painting, Modeling, Cabinet Making, Carving, Leather Work, Knowing the Trees in Winter, How to Protect the Family, At Ease on All Occasions, How to Preside at a Meeting, Home Decorating Today.

There were many surprises in the choices of classes made. "Everyday English" enrolled 166 and required two teachers. One woman said she was prompted to take this course by her son's criticism of her grammar when he came home from college. "History of Greenville" was moved to a larger room. "Recent Books and Plays" had 275. "Public Speaking" was important to 163. One hundred and twenty-one were interested in "Home Decorating."

One reason for the success of the first Citizens Education Center was the excellent newspaper and radio publicity built around the slogan, "It's Fun to Learn." Another was the support of the luncheon clubs. The novelty of the idea also helped.

Flushed with the success of this initial attempt the Citizens Education Center board decided to experiment with two terms, fall and winter, in the second year. Thirty-five courses were offered for 800 persons in the first, and 22 for 296 in the second term. In 1941, therefore, a winter term only was arranged for. The attendance was only 450, but interestingly enough a considerable majority of these persons had never enrolled before and apparently came from a lower economic group.

The high attendance the first year may have been due to interest in a new intellectual "stunt." As the novelty wore off, enrollment declined. Some courses failed to meet the expectations of the adult enrollees, partly because of the large size of classes, partly because of poor teaching. Conflicting attractions, such as a city-wide evangelistic campaign, the Community Chest drive and a new southeastern cotton festival, also reduced enrollment in the second and third years. A few of the professional teachers found that mature adults, attending voluntarily, were more exacting in their demands than college or high-school students compelled to attend. On the other hand, some of the laymen with special skills, who had never taught before, seemed to sense the needs of their groups and held them to the end. This, of course, is a familiar experience in adult education. The manual courses, while well attended did not draw as well as the lecture classes. Limited enrollment courses using the discussion method, seemed to bring the greatest satisfaction.

As already noted the idea spread successfully to four of the eight communities with local councils and also to a number of other cities in the state. With the second session, true to County Council procedure, the Citizens Education Center was turned over to a permanent organization, the Council merely remaining in a coöperative relationship. In 1942 it was operated by the city school system.

Parker District People's College.—Another urban educational venture was in the mill villages of the Parker District of metropolitan Greenville. This has been mentioned before but deserves attention because of the Southern tradition that separates the social, religious, educational, and economic life of mill villages from that of the rest of the community and because of the considerable degree of success achieved by this enterprise which, as noted earlier, was set up before the County Council but which was aided by it. The first annual report of the Greenville County Council for Community Development summarizes the program and the results for that year:

1. Of the 620 illiterates in the Parker District, 204 whites and 57 Negroes were taught to read and write.
2. Sixty-five classes in vocational education with an enrollment of 986 adults were organized. Through these classes, 225 standard cotton textile school credit cards were issued.
3. Thirty-three general adult education classes with a total enrollment of 513 students were conducted.
4. Fourteen Community Councils, of 12 leaders from each community, were organized to promote community interest and improvement.
5. Clubs—such as dramatic, travel, cooking, gardening, mothers', sewing, and home-making clubs—have been organized throughout the Parker District. These clubs have a total enrollment of 943 adults.

In subsequent years forums, courses in human relations and elementary economics, current events, home and ground beautification on a demonstration basis were added. One community bought grass seed coöperatively at a very low price, and as the grass grew purchased 125 lawn mowers at half price by pooling orders.

Four special projects of the County Council have now been described, two each concerned chiefly with the country and the metropolitan area. The two remaining special interest areas to be discussed, health and government, concerned the whole county without regard to urban and rural differences.

HEALTH

At the beginning of the Greenville County Council for Community Development experiment, the health situation in the county was complicated by two separate tax-supported health departments, one for the county, the other for the city with a combined budget of about $130,000. This set-up made for waste and duplication, the inevitable result of overlapping jurisdictions. Both of these completely separated departments were in charge of physicians with graduate training in public health. The county staff consisted of two trained sanitary inspectors and four graduate nurses. The city had a dairy and abattoir supervisor, a laboratory technician, veterinarian, one white and one Negro nurse.

A plan for coördination.—Within the first year of the Council's life the superintendent of the General Hospital proposed a plan for the coördination of the two health departments and the organization of a County Visiting Nurses Association, headquarters to be with the County Council. The city and county health departments were to furnish six nurses, and the hospital agreed to keep two senior nurses in the field. Conversations with the State, County, and City Health Departments resulted in the appointment of a supervising committee composed of the two local health officers, a member of the County Medical Association, three representatives of the State Department, and two officers of the County Council. All details were worked out. A director of health activities was added to the County Council's staff and the salary of a supervisor for the visiting nurses was secured by the Council from a foundation, supplemented by a grant from the United States Public Health Service through the State Board of Health.

Just when the program was to start, a change of county health commissioner took place. The new incumbent had been granted two additional nurses by the state and preferred to carry out his own program. It was still hoped to work out a coördinated program but a conflict situation within the

State Health Department prevented and the plan was abandoned.

Instead a demonstration program of intensive, generalized public health nursing service, on the basis of one nurse for approximately 2,000 people as against one for about 15,000 under the health department set-ups, was organized in each of three units, an urban neighborhood, an open country community, and a village. Local councils existed in the last two.

This plan was carried out as will be shown. Before its initiation the director of health activities had made a detailed study of health data for county and state with special reference to the diseases most prevalent, located for the county health department evident foci for the spread of malaria, and prepared detailed reports on sanitation for each of the 153 rural schools and those of the Parker District. A number of necessary improvements were made as a result of these surveys.

The demonstration program.—When the demonstration program got under way it included:

1. Maternity and child health, carried on by means of home visiting, and by monthly prenatal, well-baby clinics, and mothers' classes held in the center.
2. School health work, conducted with the close coöperation of the school authorities. The teachers in each district were taught by the nurse to give a daily health inspection. The nurse went to each school every morning and gave a more thorough examination to those children the teachers felt needed it. Sick children were sent home and instruction given for care. Children with defects were listed and then parents visited to stress the importance of getting the defects corrected. First aid treatments were given when necessary. Dental and immunization clinics were held in the schools periodically.
3. Communicable disease control, which consists both of quarantining contagious diseases and of teaching mode of transmis-

sion and control. The nurse taught how to take care of the patient and how to protect the rest of the family. Community immunization clinics were also held periodically.

4. Follow-up of hospital and clinic indigent cases with bedside care (under doctor's orders) when necessary. Some standing orders for the nurses' use have been approved by the County Medical Association. (No sick case is visited more than twice unless a doctor has been called.)

5. Crippled children service, which consisted of referring all crippled children to an orthopedic clinic and seeing that they got there if possible, and following out any orders that the doctor might send home with the child.

6. Health education in the form of first aid classes, mothers' classes, demonstrations of all kinds, talks, pictures, and distribution of health literature.

7. Records and reports were given to the local health committee once a month and sent to the health officer of the official agencies as well as to the Greenville County Council for Community Development.

At the outset the program was discussed with the health committees of the area councils to ascertain needs. This enabled the nurse to explain the program which a number confused with the usual bedside nursing service. It also revealed that the local committees did not know enough about conditions to advise as to local needs. House-to-house surveys were decided on. The results of these surveys were very unlooked for, in more than one way. As word of the questionnaire spread some hurriedly screened their houses, others took their children to the doctor to be vaccinated, some had their wells and privies made sanitary.

These local committees were very valuable in reporting cases of illness, the return of patients dismissed from the hospitals, and unfavorable health conditions to the nurse, in becoming better informed about community health and aid-ing the nurse in her program, especially by explaining it in the community.

When the grant for this health program was exhausted, the local people subscribed toward its continuance for a limited period, pending an effort to get the state to assume the work. It is still going on in the village, and in the urban Negro neighborhood with WPA help. The open country community now gets one day's service a week.

Permanent contribution.—The original plan to unite the city and county health departments, and to establish a coordinated county-wide public health nursing service has not been carried out. The need is still apparent. A recent Rotary Club panel discussion of problems affecting Greenville County, presented first at the club and later over the local radio station, again pointed out the financial waste from the duplication of health programs in county and state. Sufficient pressure has been brought to cause the Council of Social Agencies to undertake a scientific social study of the health area.

The demonstration nursing program has made the communities of the county health conscious. Five requests were received by the Council for public health nurses. Funds were not available, but petitions were circulated asking the County Health Commissioner to provide a nurse for each of these communities. In addition to this four communities have provided nursing centers in their high-school buildings which are served one day a week by one of the county nurses.

The desirability of having county public health nurses "in residence" in the areas served was proven. Local health committees have been found to be effective in maintaining contacts between visiting nurses and community need.

ECONOMICS AND GOVERNMENT

One of the interests of the foundation which appropriated the funds for the five-year experiment in county-wide community development was to see if one result might not be some improvement in the crazy quilt pattern which local government has come to assume all over rural America. To this end a political scientist was appointed to the college faculty with the understanding that he should also serve as consultant on the staff of the County Council.

Within a few months after the inception of the project the Executive Committee of the Council decided to appoint a general committee of 16 on Commerce and Government. For the most part the persons selected were chosen because of the official positions they held. The committee included the editor of a local paper, the publisher of the two local papers, the presidents of four of the luncheon clubs, the secretary of the Chamber of Commerce, the dean of girls at the city high school, the superintendent of the Parker District schools, the chairman of the county legislative delegation, a member of the city council, the chairman of the board of county commissioners, the secretary of that board, the county superintendent of education, a lawyer, a textile executive, and the wife of a former textile executive.

This was the first committee appointed by the Council. It will be noted that there was no demand for it from the constituency, and that no tasks recognized by a number of people awaited doing. In this important respect it differed from the county and local health committees described in the preceding section. On the other hand the Executive Committee felt an obligation to the foundation to move quickly into this area of interest.

Under the circumstances it was not surprising that only half of the 16 members attended the first meeting or that half of the membership resigned before the end of the Council's first year. Some of them had little interest in or understanding of the project. Some of them were a bit afraid of the possible implications of the project. One of the officials appointed to the committee took the interesting position that he as a public official could have nothing to do with the public in this sort of project. Others of this group appeared to pay lip service to coöperation but to act as if they held membership in the committee to make sure that nothing was done.

The consultant moved with proper caution. He suggested as first steps a number of possible studies, such as of governmental costs in comparison with similar cities and counties, and of the city's traffic problems; on the action side, he suggested the obtaining of street markers for the city, a clean-up of city newsstands, and a series of public forums or discussions on the functions and services of various branches of government.

These were obviously quite new ideas to the committee. It discussed them gingerly, agreed that something should be done, but took no action except the election of a chairman and co-chairman, neither of whom ever functioned.

Some of the Council's Executive Committee urged that the Council make haste slowly in matters of government especially since they believed nothing could be done until there had been sweeping changes in the personnel of local public offices. In this latter contention they were doubtless correct. The committee was therefore reconstituted and put major stress on economic problems. Some of the projects already described in this report were first discussed in its sessions but government, despite the talk about its being a really important feature in the Council program, despite statements about its significance to the future of planning in the county, was shelved.

In spite of that, the staff did their best with individuals and small interested groups. The traffic survey was made by students, as described in a previous chapter, and its recommendations put into effect. Interest was kept alive in city zoning, which is now becoming a reality. The library forums dealing with international and national affairs were carried on through one fall and winter with capacity crowds. Discussions on "Southern Regions and Greenville County's Place in the South" and "Taxation" enrolled 70 and 20 persons respectively. Innumerable talks were made to women's clubs, civic clubs, and other organizations on governmental problems. A four-day institute on local government was held which brought specialists from all over the South. Platforms were drafted for candidates for local office. A Good Government Association was formed to campaign behind the scenes in the coming city and county elections, the hope being that the needed changes in governmental personnel might be effected. They were.

At that point it seemed as if the way had opened to take up the program, but the lay leadership of the Council took the position that because "good men" were now in office, they could be relied upon "to do what was right." The Committee on Government was politely invited to keep out of the way and did.

Probably most community organizations other than those specifically political in aims would have made a similar decision. It would be defended on the ground that such an agency should be politically neutral. Apart from the fact that the Council or at least some of its lay leadership had not been neutral, the theory behind this contention is debatable. A community organization has every right in a democracy to speak its mind to those in authority on issues that concern the community as a whole and which by that token are largely removed from political partisanship. Indeed, it has an obligation to do just this. The very pose of neutrality is one reason why some agencies never get beyond the stage of discussions and pleasant recreations. The County Council for Community Development lost its most important battles in this area. The housing project failed to materialize at first though now assured. The park for Negroes was not voted. The creation of a County Planning Board was defeated. In each case the support seemed adequate. Community organizers must learn not only to work with all the people, democratically. They must also learn to work with those who have political power because it has been delegated to them by the suffrage of the people and to work in such a way that the power inherent in adequate community organization comes to be apparent and to be respected.

In the case of the Greenville County Council for Community Development, apart from the indication already given for these outcomes of the work of the committee on economics and government, the complexity of the problems may have discouraged the participation of some.

The varying tasks of the reconstituted committee brought a number of the staff members into relation with it which may have confused some of its members. The work in this area was more hampered than that in some others by traditions and vested interests. This situation would seem to have called for a more continuous and thoroughgoing educational effort than was put forward and more attempt to inform and educate public officials as to the objectives and possibilities of the County Council. Had this been done the strongly supported proposal to turn the Council into a tax-supported County Planning Board at the expiration of the foundation grant might have been more cordially received by officials. It must also be stated that in the governmental area there was more severe competition than in some others between the interests of the college and the classroom on the one hand and the Council on the other.

CHAPTER VII

Development in the Negro Area[1]

THERE ARE MANY unpleasant facts regarding the place of the Negro in American life that must be faced by members of both races. These stem from a history which none now living had any share in making but which condition any program of community development of which the Negro is a part.

Negroes are a minority group in America and for a number of reasons they do not share equally in the community life in any part of the nation. Consequently they do not feel that they have full freedom to participate in community enterprises. The situation of the Negro minority in America is one of those in which the American democratic ideal still lacks much of attainment.

This fact is regrettable but real. No program of community development for Negroes can be planned completely and immediately in accordance with the theory of American democratic idealism. Any progress for the Negro group must start from the situation in which the Negro is, or be foredoomed to failure.

To give a true account of the Negroes' participation in the program of the Greenville County Council for Community Development and to evaluate the principles and methods of procedure adopted by the Council with reference to the Negro group, factors of population and its racial proportions, economic resources, attitudes of the Negro group toward its

---

1. Much of this chapter was written by R. O. Johnson, M.A., Negro Coördinator.

status and improvement, and the potential leadership within the group must be taken into account. Some of these are given in Chapter I.

Another factor is the relation of the dominant to the weaker "caste." As the efforts of the Negro group as a part of the Council are viewed retrospectively, the factor of caste and class looms as an important determinant of attitudes and of the degree of participation of both whites and Negroes in any effort to improve the status of the latter. When faced with the question of improving conditions among Negroes, a member of the dominant group is forced by the usage of society to think first of what will be the reaction of his group to any act on his part in behalf of the weaker group. Likewise, a member of the weaker group will think first of what will be the reaction not of his group, but of the dominant group to any efforts on his part for the improvement of his group. The needs and welfare of the weaker group thus become subordinate to the thinking of the dominant group. The Negro work of the Greenville County Council must, therefore, be viewed against the background of this social pattern.

It should be remembered that the Council is not a group coming in from the outside. It is rather a group of approximately 200 Greenville County residents plus a small staff of trained workers, for the most part residents of the county. The idea was conceived by Greenville people and is controlled and directed by Greenville residents. The Council seeks to serve as a stimulus that will set the people of the county to working out their own problems in their own way. The Council thinks of itself as having no program to put over in the county. It assumes its task to be that of a co-ordinating agency. Conference and research are vital parts of its method.

How was the Negro as a special group integrated in this

program? From the beginning the Council had a Committee on Interracial Coöperation. This committee was composed of approximately twelve members of the Council and approximately the same number of Negroes selected on the basis of their standing in the community, together with two Negro members of the Council staff, a registered nurse, and a young man who taught community singing in a number of Negro communities. There was also a white staff adviser of the committee who rendered a wide variety of services to the Negro group during the first two years of the Council's existence.

Among the activities of this committee in which white staff members assisted were the establishment of an adult school in a Negro community which majored on adult elementary and vocational education broadly conceived, the furnishing of lecturers, teachers and materials for WPA adult education teachers, NYA recreational leaders, and for Negro day schoolteachers, the demonstration of games for adults at various Negro schools, the organization of a small library on progressive education methods for teachers, and the advisement of the Negro Center in the city of Greenville.

The adult school alluded to deserves further mention. It was initiated at the suggestion of the Negro school principal. After a number of conferences with county school officials a Negro "Adult College" was organized. The curriculum covered agriculture, farm and home mechanics, home making and English. Before classes began the local schoolteachers who conducted them were given special training in adult education and learning by staff members of the Greenville County Council for Community Development. Content of the courses was determined by the problems the students listed as important to them. The project method and discussion techniques were largely used in the classes. The students in farm mechanics, for instance, did most of their work in the community, building brick flues, roofing and screening houses, constructing hog lots and houses and replacing window panes. The home-making group gave simple parties, made inexpensive washstands and dressing tables, studied child feeding and the planning, preparation, and serving of meals. Project and demonstration methods were similarly used in the other classes. Some materials of instruction were furnished by the County Council.

The "college" met weekly for three months during the winter in the school building. There were two fifty-minute periods at the end of which a very popular recreational and athletic program was conducted. The enrollment the first year was 75, of whom 63 were awarded perfect attendance certificates. Each enrollee paid 50c which with Smith-Hughes law allotments for adult teachers was sufficient to cover expenses.

At the request of the County Board of Education the whole staff surveyed the buildings and grounds of the Negro schools. This resulted in great improvements in many of these financed in part by the county and in part by the Rosenwald Fund. Conditions among the Negro blind were also surveyed and some rehabilitation was accomplished. Surveys of Negro housing and social problems were also made, assisted by students of the college and by upper-class students in the Negro high school.

The health director made no difference between the races in his program. The Negro nurse carried a very full program of bedside visits, clinics, clean-ups,[2] lecturing, classes, and charitable work. The other Negro worker organized or coached a community chorus, glee club, several quartettes and orchestras, and put much emphasis on community singing.

2. One minor feature of this program resulted in the removal of 52,685 discarded tin cans of various sizes in seven neighborhoods by school children for prizes of one peanut per can. Local merchants and friends supplied the peanuts, the local supply of which was temporarily exhausted.

This chapter will deal chiefly with Negro activities beginning with the third year of the Council's program at which time the coördinator of Negro activities was employed. This step was taken in the belief that the Negro work could be done more effectively in this way than under the plan first tried.

Primarily, it was the duty of the county coördinator to work with the Negro group following the basic principles and methods of procedure adopted by the Council with reference to the white population and embodied in the slogan: "Helping people to help themselves." Consideration was, of course, given to the social, economic, and cultural differences of the two groups. To coördinate the work of Negro agencies in the city and county and to serve as a liaison agent between the Council and its Negro division were part of the duties.

The first steps taken by the Negro county coördinator involved a study of the work of the first two years, getting acquainted with the Negro people, their attitudes toward the Council program, their own organizations and their programs, their social groups and classes and the ideas of these toward existing conditions and toward coöperation for the improvement of these conditions. Coöperative relationships were developed with the Negro agents serving on a county-wide basis—the Home Demonstration Agent, the Farm Agent, the Jeanes Supervisor, and the librarian. As a newcomer, one apart from all parties and factions, it was relatively easy to get a frank expression of opinion on most subjects on which the coördinator desired information.

A survey of the city of Greenville was made and a basic map developed to show all Negro streets, churches, schools, places of amusement, and vacant plots of land which might be secured for recreational areas. Thus many insights into the life of the people were gained.

As has already been noted from Chapter I, over half of the Negro population of the county was in metropolitan Greenville. Most of these people were recent migrants, which made their problems more difficult. Nearly a third were in the southern half as were one half of the 62 Negro schools, including the four or five offering vocational home economics and agriculture. In this southern half of the county the bulk of the work of the Negro agents listed above was concentrated.

The Home Demonstration and Farm Agents were given office space in the same room with the county coördinator which enhanced the possibility of coöperative planning and coördination of programs between these three agents. The librarian who serves both the city and county entered fully into the program of coördination. A degree of coöperation was secured from the Jeanes Supervisor. From the beginning the Extension Service was closely tied up with the Council program. Perhaps because of this, difficulty was experienced later in bringing the vocational teachers into full coöperation, there being a long-standing conflict between the State Extension Service and the State (Smith-Hughes) vocational education division. As time went on the degree of coöperation increased.

Helping people to help themselves.—With the facts gathered and relationships established the next step was to make the initial test of the idea of helping people to help themselves. A group of people representing a cross-section of the thinking and occupations of the Negroes of the county and the various agents was convened to discuss informally some of the needs and problems of their communities and the steps involved in satisfying these needs. Several problems presented themselves at this point, such as selecting the group, securing a free and frank discussion, and how in the light of it and the somewhat unpleasant situation faced by the Negroes, to stimulate and maintain an attitude of open-mindedness, optimism, and a desire for action.

Selecting leaders.—Such a nucleus group seemed necessary. The democratic process had been accepted as a basic factor in the Council's method of procedure. There were no community organizations representative of a majority of the people that could be asked to send representatives to this meeting. The persons were, therefore, picked from fifty-one school communities of the county, an effort being made to get recognized leaders from all walks of life.

Forty-three persons attended this meeting. After discussion an organization was formed, patterned largely after the parent organization—the white Council. With the lack of experience of the people in doing things for themselves or accepting community responsibilities, and their lack of faith that anything could release them from the traditional controls which have prevented them from exercising their initiative collectively for their welfare, many could not envision an organization operating on a county-wide basis. To these the principles and policies adopted seemed much more practical if applied to individual communities. However, most of the persons attending this meeting pledged themselves to go back to their respective communities and attempt to stimulate in their neighbors an interest in the problems of their respective communities and the possibilities of the Council procedure as a means for doing something about these problems.

As with the white Council this procedure in forming the Negro Council was not wholly democratic, though its meetings certainly were, and with the limited staff and time no other method was feasible. Not all those originally selected coöperated, some from inability to lead, some because of being too busy. But within a year the Council was functioning and those who could lead their communities to the attainments of objectives by coöperative work had been discovered and enlisted.

In this year also the basic philosophies, objectives, and methods of procedure were tested and finally determined.

Seven communities begin.—Seven communities took the idea seriously; a series of community meetings were called at which general discussions on needs and problems of the community took place. These meetings were aimed at stimulating interest in community welfare. The county coördinator usually acted as discussion leader, but not as chairman or promoter of the meeting. This was always done by some interested person, preferably a recognized leader of the community, who accepted the responsibility days in advance of the meeting. No attempt to form a local organization was made until a sizeable proportion of the people of the community understood the plan.

As soon as the first meetings agreed on a problem those most interested made a study of it. Here the county coördinator would lend his assistance in helping to find the facts. These gathered, a solution to the discovered problems was sought. This was the crucial point, for the failure to make some degree of progress would invariably mean the loss of some supporters. The set-backs which resulted from failure to achieve some of the first goals set forced those who had to steer these organizations to adopt a policy of selecting for first consideration those projects which had more than a fair chance of succeeding. By succeeding in several small undertakings the group morale was built up so it could stand the strain of failure or extremely slow and often interrupted progress which was frequent in the case of larger projects. Thus the experience of the Negro Council validated one of the most important principles of community organization: to create a psychology of success.

The story of some of these centers appears later in the chapter.

The first year.—During the first year the county coördinator gave regular assistance to nine communities, rural and urban, along the lines described, of conference, fact-finding, and action. Organization was the necessary mechanism for carrying on this work. The complexity of organization varied according to the size of the community and the nature of its problems. In every instance an effort was made to keep the organization in its organizational structure as simple as possible.

Only in metropolitan Greenville was the organization divided into standing committees each functioning in a restricted capacity. The rural organizations which were of the neighborhood type operated as one large committee working on one problem at a time.

Organizing the Greenville Area Council.—Organization of the Greenville Area Council in the city was completed in November of 1938 after six weekly conferences in which most of the problems of the community were discussed. The membership reached sixty-three during the first year. The acuteness and complexity of the city's problems and the fact that the municipal government and a few other agencies dealt with some of them resulted in the formation of standing committees which would concentrate on specific problems and work with the proper authorities in order that the Negro might be included in all programs. These committees were concerned with education, leisure time and recreation, health, crime and delinquency, government and economics. Committee recommendations made after study, were brought back to the Council for action by the whole group. If any problem seemed beyond the power of the Negro group to solve it was referred to the white Council in order to secure the support of this body. Projects carried out wholly by the Negro Council often had the advice of the white coördinator and were always reported to the County Council. In this way coördination of activities of the two divisions of the Greenville County Council was reasonably well maintained.

THE WORK OF THE GREENVILLE AREA COUNCIL

Recreation.—The committee on recreation first studied the "Report on Recreation in Greenville County in 1936" by R. D. Bailey, of the National Park Service, alluded to earlier. This report described the recreational facilities for both races in Greenville County in 1936 and proposed long-time improvement programs. The second step was to study the situation in metropolitan Greenville, visiting the school grounds, observing children at play on vacant lots and in the streets. It next surveyed the situation in some cities which had provided more adequate recreational opportunities for Negroes than Greenville. Using the County Coördinator's base map already described, the committee drew up a proposal for beginning a public recreational program for the Negro population of Greenville. It recommended the purchase of land for a park of 27 acres and the development of five Negro neighborhood playgrounds at the schools. The purchase of land for the park was recommended for first consideration as available sites for this purpose were fast being developed for other purposes.

The findings of the committee with its recommendations were submitted to the Park and Tree Commission and the City Department of Recreation. Both of these endorsed the recommendations which were then submitted to the Municipal Council by the Negro Council with the support of the above two governmental agencies and the Greenville County Council. Unfortunately efforts to secure purchase of the land failed.

Other attempts were made in various ways to get some favorable action. Each failed, but Negro recreational needs were thus brought before the public. Finally a survey of recreational facilities for Negroes in 26 cities of the Southeast was made and findings submitted to the Department of Recreation and the City Board of Education. This study showed a definite trend toward a greater use of school facilities for recreational purposes. As a result of this study and two years of efforts to get something done about the recreational needs of the Negro groups in Greenville, an agreement was reached between the City Board of Education and the City Council in the spring of 1940 to allow the latter to develop playgrounds at three of the schools of the city.

In the meantime, the Negro Council undertook other projects. Through the coöperation of the recently established Catholic Church the five acres surrounding the church were developed fairly adequately as a playground with swings, slide, tennis court, horse-shoes, basketball, boxing, and with space for basketball, softball, and football. Installation of one large spot light made it possible to carry on some activities at night. One year of operation of this playground has demonstrated its value. Three neighborhood play lots have been operated with very limited facilities with the help of the WPA and volunteer assistance. The committee is still working to secure more recreational facilities for the Negro group and to make the public more conscious of the leisure time problem. Valuable assistance in this was secured from the Director of Negro Work of the National Recreational Association.

Education.—The committee on education made a study of the attitude toward minority groups revealed in the textbooks used in public schools of the county. It showed that little which would tend to inspire Negro children has been included in any of these books. Definite action followed.

Recommendations were made to persons in charge of purchasing books for the Negro library that more books by and about Negroes be included in future purchases. As a result, more than 200 volumes of the best books on the Negro were purchased for the library in 1940. Through the efforts of this committee approximately 2,000 volumes were secured for the city high school from the Faith Cabin Library Movement.

Each year two or three public programs featuring some outstanding speaker are given. Public forums, band concerts, and community singing are part of the educational program of the Council. Assistance has been given to the two nursery schools operated by the WPA.

Health.—The committee on health has conducted clean-up campaigns using volunteer workers. These have reached every section of the city in varying degrees. This program was started as a part of the observance of the National Negro Health Movement in 1939 and repeated in 1940. It is destined to become an annual feature. It includes essay and health poster contests conducted in the schools, health programs, radio programs, health movies, clinics, and public health lectures.

Crime and delinquency.—The committee on crime and delinquency has made a study of these two aspects of Greenville life for the period from 1928 to 1938. Facts revealed by these studies have been printed on large charts which have served as a basis of discussion for a series of forums on Crime, Its Causes and Costs. Close coöperation with the Juvenile Court has been maintained with mutual benefits to both the people and the court. Efforts are being made to secure an Opportunity Farm for Negroes which would offer various useful activities for boys and thus aid in the drive to curb delinquency in Greenville.

Economics and government.—The committees on economics and government have jointly conducted a series of studies. The first, in coöperation with the County Council staff, explored living conditions in one Negro slum area. Support to the NYA Training Center for Girls is one of the tangible accomplishments of this committee. Information was gathered on federal housing projects in seven cities of the Southeast when it seemed that Greenville might get one. A survey of the effect of the federal wages and hours law on Greenville Negroes was made, as was one on the democratic primary and poll tax laws in the South.

The Council restudies its procedure.—The failure of the Greenville City Negro Council to attain some of its objectives in its first year led to a reappraisal of its procedures. Replies to inquiries sent to the Chambers of Commerce of 46 cities indicated a majority conviction that the most effective Negro organization is a local branch of the National Urban League. The League and many of its branches were then asked for information. Conference followed. The League, it developed, requires its locals to be bi-racial. This reenforced the basic conclusion of the Greenville City Negro Council that the unsupported efforts of a Negro agency are too often passed by in the rush of other business by public authorities or construed, often mistakenly, as the demands of small pressure groups.

After much deliberation the Negro Council saw the desirability of changing its procedures and of a more permanent organization through affiliation with the Urban League. This was accomplished early in 1940. As a result findings and petitions do not originate in one group and pass to the other. The persons of the white race, who in the last analysis determine whether or not a thing is done, have a part in the procedure from beginning to end. The existence of the two councils made the transition fairly easy.

Suburban Greenville.—Four Negro neighborhoods or communities in the suburban area of Greenville, two of them textile mill villages, have been organized. The programs have been relatively simple, including health, clean-ups, gardening, home improvement, and assistance to the school. In one case the neighborhood council serves as P.T.A. In another where there is no Negro institution save a one-room school, the organization's program includes devotional services and indoor and outdoor games. In one of these cases the Negro group morale was very low. But by perseverance a considerable number of parents were brought to the school to observe the work of their children in a newly introduced "activity" program. It was explained that one reason for this educational method as against recitations only was that it taught children both to do things for themselves and to work together in groups. At the end of the evening a parent raised the question of an adult club associated with the school, the program of which has slowly but steadily broadened. The secret of success here, as stated by one Negro parent, gave also another cardinal principle of community organization, phrased as follows: "We've been taught how to do things we all want to do, not told what we must do."

Some of the most significant work of the Negro Council was done not in metropolitan Greenville and its suburbs but in the rural part of the county.

Laurel Creek.—This community was important to the work of the Negro Council because it was one of two in the rural part of the county which had received assistance before the appointment of the Negro coördinator. It was, therefore, of high interest to those who gathered to consider the proposed Negro Council to know how these ideas had benefited Laurel Creek. It was located near the center of the county, had a good school and a slightly higher proportion of home owners, one in four, than other Negro centers. All of the 85 families were engaged in farming. There were two churches.

Early in the first year of the Greenville County Council for Community Development a socio-economic survey had been made of the community by the local school, and on the basis of the facts discovered a number of activities had been initiated, especially in the improvement of teaching and in making the school more community centered. Though little assistance was given in the following year the alert school principal continued most of the activities.

The Negro coördinator began by helping this principal with some of his immediate problems such as getting more materials for the school. Others, such as securing an adequate water supply for the school and improving its grounds and stimulating a home improvement program, were referred to the local Council made up of parents, out-of-school youth, and pupils of the upper grades who were organized as an Improvement Club.

The club, the spearhead of several movements for community betterment, made a socio-economic survey in order to compare the situation in 1938 with that shown by the first study in 1936. It covered health, recreation, religious activities, living conditions and standards in some detail. The results were recorded on two color charts placed on the wall of the assembly hall and became the core of the school curriculum and the guide for all activities of the Community Council.

The program for the community taken up item by item as decided by the group has included screening of houses, planting year-round gardens, canning, securing electricity, building sanitary toilets, wider use of public health facilities, community recreation, and encouraging diversified farming. The program for the school has included enlarging school grounds, digging of a well, repair of building, improvement of instruction, increasing number of books in library, and extension of school term.

During a conference for educational leaders of the state sponsored by the State Department of Education and the General Education Board in April, 1938, students from this school gave a discussion on making a survey of our community which created such interest that on invitation 12 of the students visited six schools and conducted similar discussions before the upper classes.

Although similar results could not be reasonably expected in every community of Greenville County, the achievement is significant. It shows, first of all, the value of home ownership, and secondly the practicability of the Council philosophy and procedure in a rural area.

Seven other Negro neighborhoods or communities were organized, six of them in the southern half of the county. The work in these six was coördinated with that of the Home Demonstration and County Agricultural Agents since all were in the areas they most frequently visited. Moreover it was hoped that by this coördination and experience these agents would be the better equipped to take over the rural community work when the foundation grant expired.

The record here set forth of Negro success and failure in community organization contains much of encouragement for leaders of the race. The situation in Greenville was not of the best when the experiment began, and the program did not accomplish all that was hoped. Some of its failures have been noted in this chapter. Others occurred which have not been mentioned. There were problems of keeping the leaders at work, of combatting individual and group discouragement and indifference, and often these were not solved. But the record of achievements is impressive. These have been stressed to show that under trained leadership the

Negro minority did make progress in an attack on its problems. Negro morale improved according to the testimony
of many of the race. For the future, of course, much depends
on the new organizational set-up and, in the rural areas, on
the ability of the extension agents and vocational teachers to
carry on the projects started.

CHAPTER VIII

Conclusions

IT HAD BEEN hoped both by the Foundation which gave the five-year grant and by the local leaders in Greenville who applied for it, that the County Council for Community Development would sufficiently commend itself to the people of the county that some means would be found to continue it at the expiration of the grant without further subsidy. This was stated by the General Education Board. It was stated at the first meeting of the Council after the grant had been made. It was reiterated during the entire five-year period.

Various plans were discussed as to how this might be accomplished. One was to finance the Council through the Community Chest. Another was to attempt the underwriting of the budget independently. A third was to continue the planning and initiating functions as a tax-supported County Planning Board. Opinion finally crystallized behind the last-mentioned plan, but as noted in Chapter VI the authorities refused to agree to this despite strong support.

The plan finally adopted provides that some of the Council's functions shall be taken over by various county agencies and by departments of the local college. The Council program in modified form is continuing to function with staff provided on a part-time basis by the college, some of the county agencies, and a small two-year grant from the sponsoring foundation.

The rest of this chapter is devoted first of all to some comments on the failure to achieve a full-fledged continuance of the Council on something like its basis of operation during its last two years. Attention is then given to some of the Council's outstanding achievements and finally some observations are set down concerning the experience of the Council that may be of value to the general field of community organization.

WHY THE COUNCIL FAILED OF FULL CONTINUANCE

When one takes up the first of these matters, the reasons why the Council failed of full continuance, it must frankly be admitted that one enters in part the area of speculation. Motives cannot be analyzed with laboratory exactness and motives certainly played a part, for the county had the resources to support the organization if one compares its total welfare and charitable budget with its resources and with the ratio of such gifts to resources in other communities. This is in part made clear from the analysis in Chapter I.

Fear of Council's potential power.—One of the motives that entered into the eventual fate of the Council may have been fear. In a number of particulars it had demonstrated real power. It had been partly responsible for a change in elected government personnel. It was therefore a potential threat to the security of office holders with their own organizations. Had it continued to live and grow in power it might have made life less comfortable for City Hall and the County Court House. It had probably been a considerable nuisance to those buildings on several occasions. It had demonstrated in both the Cotton Discussion and Live-at-Home programs that it could organize the rural areas for action. Its very success therefore may have aroused some subconscious opposition. Direct evidence to support this supposition is lacking. It was probably not more than a minor factor, but the possibility of its operation cannot be ruled out of account especially since it is a theory of some of the county's leaders.

Opposition to inter-racial policies.—Another element of fear that may have entered into the picture was the Council's work in the Negro area, described in Chapter VII. It is known that some persons were disturbed by its advocacy of playground and recreational space for this large but minority group. Despite the endorsement of this proposal by other important bodies, including two official commissions, the City Council turned it down and this decision must have been advocated by some groups or citizens of influence. As in many Southern cities there is a branch of the Ku Klux Klan in Greenville. The inter-racial issue even flared up within the Council itself at one point and resulted in a serious difference of opinion between some of the staff and a few members of the Executive Committee, some effects of which were a handicap to the end of the experiment.

Conflict over housing.—Whether or not these fears were operative, the Council did gain the opposition and possibly the enmity of some. Its advocacy of a slum-clearance housing project, which initially missed consummation by a narrow margin and which is now to become a reality may have been an important factor in this opposition. Greenville was not peculiar with respect to opposition to such projects, and it is quite natural that those who fought federally aided housing were distrustful of those who initiated the project.

Looking back it is easy to say according to one's point of view, that if the Council had been more courageous or more cautious at this or that point both these projects and its future might have met a different fate. Just so one can claim that if the United States had joined the League of Nations or if England and France had supported Czechoslovakia in 1938, there would have been no Second World War. Precise analysis in the realm of speculation is impossible without possession of all the facts, including those that lie buried deep in the hearts of men.

Early disagreement within Council.—But there are other considerations relative to the Council's work and fate that lie within its own area of operation and that an analysis that attempts objectivity must record with frankness. As stated in the opening pages of this report, the project was a hybrid. It was a fusion of four sets of ideas. Some though not all of the original sponsors and staff members had pretty well-defined opinions as to what the project should be and do. There developed a clash between those who knew what to do and wanted it done and those who wished the Council to discover and build its program out of a growing knowledge of the conditions and needs of the county. This difference in viewpoint was so serious that for some months in the first year no staff meetings were held and finally three members of the staff resigned. As a result much precious time was lost at the very outset and the form and philosophy of the Council was not set until well into the second year after the coming of the new coördinator.

The original membership of the Council was quite small for a county and a project so large. Its enlargement and step-by-step education of the membership was a matter of the last three years and was accomplished only after a certain amount of resistance was overcome. The transition from the usual type of executive control and leadership which characterizes much of the economic and social organization of America to a democratic basis is not achievable in a day or a year. Democracy is a process, not merely a technique of administration, but that fact is not readily recognized and the value of that process takes time to demonstrate.

Forcing social change.—Five years is not a long time. Social habits change slowly and leaders in that change who pin their faith in the democratic process must possess a fine balance of impatience that spurs them to achievement and patience that makes them sympathetic to, and understanding of, the habits and mores they seek to change. It cannot be demonstrated that if the Council had had seven instead of five years it would have succeeded. That also is supposition but the support for it lies in the story of growing achievement this report has told. Usual Foundation policy is to limit grants to three or five years. There are sound reasons for this but in the difficult realm of community organization and development, which in effect is the realm of social change, good administrative judgment has more than once conflicted unfortunately with sound social sense. It may have in this instance.

Inter-organizational friction.—It was implicit in the plan for the Council that it would be a fact-finding, stimulating, planning, coördinating body and hence that it would put little emphasis on its own activities. This was not completely achieved. As already noted there were those who felt enough facts were known to begin at once to operate. There never was, therefore, an initial study of the entire county shared in by the people of the county and requested by leaders who felt a lack of information and used as an educative and programizing device. This procedure was followed with considerable success in some of the local councils but what few early studies the Council made on a county basis were topical and related to particular problems. The urge to action, the desire to make a showing, resulted, especially in the first year, in publicity for various activities initiated by the Council that magnified it as an entity, despite the fact that the somewhat grandiose first annual report declared that the philosophy of the Council was to operate a project "by, of and for the people of Greenville County."

This philosophy was never abandoned even in the first year. Sometimes, however, it was eclipsed. The Council faced here a familiar dilemma of all coördinating agencies. It had to make the county conscious of its presence and its potentialities for use, and yet it had to keep from trespassing on the prerogatives and territories of existing agencies. Moreover its every move could be interpreted as an implied suggestion that some group or agency had not seen a task that needed doing. Even though the consistent policy of the Council was to ask with reference to any project: "What persons, groups, or agencies have a stake in this matter?", it was frequently found that several were concerned and "credit" became a divided matter with each concerned seeking its full share. This was especially true in the metropolitan area where over-organization had produced overlapping and duplication.

It was no accident that the Council's most satisfying and fruitful achievements were in the rural areas which had few agencies and in one or two fields where preliminary study by all concerned brought an awareness of problems needing solution so pressing that the will to coöperative action was easily aroused. Whether upwards of a year spent in a coöperative self-survey of the county under Council auspices would have prevented some of the problems outlined in this section is again a matter of speculation. To the author it appears that it would have operated in this direction and furnished a sounder basis for the program of the remaining years of the project.

Provincialism of county.—Despite the progressiveness of Greenville there was sufficient provincialism to handicap the Council on the ground that two or three staff members were "outsiders." It was felt that Greenville did not need the "help" of outsiders, and some elements criticized the Executive Committee for employing them. Among other centers of this feeling was a portion of the political group in the county. Added to this was the difficulty that the staff members at best could be known by only a small proportion of the people of the county and initially to only a few of the leaders.

Program overambitious.—It is probable that too many enterprises were undertaken for the size of the staff, especially such members of it as were carrying from half-time to practically full-time teaching loads at the college.

There were other weaknesses in the Council structure and operation more minor in character which will be dealt with in the final section of this chapter. The account turns now to a summary of the major contributions which the Council may claim to have made. These will be itemized without a recapitulation of the evidence, most of which has been given in previous chapters.

ACHIEVEMENTS OF THE COUNCIL

There is much testimony from persons of all types in the county that the major contribution of the Council has been in arousing the interest of communities in solving their own problems and in demonstrating ways in which solutions could be reached. It has demonstrated the value, not to say necessity, of an educational approach to such problems in the effecting of social change.

The Council has brought the Greenville public to a realization of the need for greatly improved social welfare, health, and recreational services for the Negro minority group and of the relation between the weaknesses in such services and the problems and costs of delinquency, crime, communicable disease and the like. It has furnished a means which the men and women of understanding and good will in interracial matters, who are to be found in increasing numbers all over the South, could use to help solve some of the problems of this minority group. More important, it has demonstrated that the Negro community, despite its disadvantaged position, possessed the leadership and vision to work by democratic means for its own benefit and it has provided for a permanent basis for the continuance of the Negro Council's work, at least in the metropolitan area, through the affiliation with the National Urban League.

A definite growth in understanding of social welfare needs and a consciousness of the need for coördination and coöperation of welfare services grew out of the Council's work. A real spirit of coöperation has developed among the agencies and the agency personnel which may result in an integrated program. Professional personnel has developed with the conscious realization of the need for trained leadership. The actual services have improved, as has the financial support. Expert consultants have been called in by several groups, and programs have been modified as a result. Closer coöperation between public and private agencies has developed. Greenville has come to be recognized throughout South Carolina as outstanding in community organization and social welfare. Specifically the Council has been a major though not the only factor in the organization of the Council of Social Agencies, the Family Welfare Society, the Legal Aid Clinic, and the Mental Hygiene Society and in the improvement of the Juvenile Court, hospital, public health and library services, and in social welfare coöperation. A thoroughgoing survey of the entire set-up of public and private, white and Negro welfare agencies, urged by the Council almost since its inception, has been made and was reported upon as this report was being written. It is very likely to result in further progress. The pattern of welfare organization and operation in Greenville will live longer than its parent and holds much of instructive value for the medium-sized cities of the South.

The Council has greatly assisted the coöperative movement through the pilgrimage of a dozen local leaders to Nova Scotia and the holding of a regional conference on coöperatives; and through the organization of coöperatives and co-operative credit unions in city and country it has demonstrated that this movement can meet successfully problems inherent in Southern conditions.

The Council has been influential in stimulating integrated advances in the field of education. Teachers, trustees, and principals have been brought together and planning and action have resulted. City and county white school systems have worked together and have coöperated with the Negro system which has been aided in various ways. The Citizens' Education Center is making a continuing contribution and the idea has not only spread to other places but is now being promoted by the Extension Division of the State University.

City and country relations and mutual understanding have been greatly improved. Five per cent of the initial Council membership was rural. At the end the rural group had its proportionate share. City and country leaders have shared in one another's problems and experiences in committees and in Council meetings, and mutual respect, not to say friendship, has developed. Unfortunately the same success was not achieved in bringing in those in the textile villages.

The Live-at-Home and other programs and the organization of local community councils, some of them with well-rounded programs, has raised the standard of living of the rural population on both its material and intangible sides.

The Council has stimulated greater interest in government, both local and that of larger units. With the coöperation in specific projects of various state and federal agencies, citizens have become more conscious of the importance, functions, and potential contributions of these agencies and have learned to request the appropriate agency for needed coöperation.

The Council has shown that when the proper coördinating agency exists it is easy to secure resources in leadership and even money from state and national organizations. A partial list of agencies and organizations that coöperated with the Council through measurable contributions of time or money includes 15 divisions, bureaus, and offices of the federal government, seven state government agencies, 13 national and five state private organizations. In addition there were coöperative relationships on one or more projects with over 60 public and private agencies in the county and city. A situation like this makes possible the marshalling of the county resources, especially on problems that are state-wide or regional.

Furman University—the local college—has become a real factor in community life and has worked out interesting devices for a broader training for its students especially in the fields of sociology and education. Students in these fields are gladly accepted as volunteer leaders or interns in all social welfare agencies, in rural communities, and in churches. Sociology majors have done excellent work at graduate and professional social work schools and many of these have returned to South Carolina and are employed by the welfare agencies of the county and throughout the state. Similarly the education majors are recognized leaders in their schools.

Finally the Council has already made many contributions to thinking and some to practice in the areas of its work beyond the boundaries of the county itself. This is attested by the increasing stream of visitors, already mentioned,[1] and the even larger stream of letters of inquiry.

It is attested also by the selection for three consecutive years of Greenville County as the locale for a summer field course in Southern conditions offered by Columbia University but taught by one of the Council staff; by the selection of Furman University, wholly because of its tie-up with the

1. In one year there were over 2,000 visitors in the schools of the Parker District alone. Many if not most of these also became somewhat acquainted with the Council. The Council itself has kept no complete record of its visitors, but they have come from those interested in all its fields of activity.

Council, as one of the 34 institutions to coöperate in the five-year program of the Commission on Teacher Education of the American Council on Education; and by the holding of a foundation-subsidized Workshop in Community Organization for 50 selected leaders in 1941, conducted by the Council and largely manned by its staff. In view then of these achievements and of the critique with which the chapter opened what are some of the implications of this experiment for community organization?

IMPLICATIONS FOR COMMUNITY ORGANIZATION[2]

Some of the implications for community organization here set down contain nothing new to specialists in this field. They simply reinforce what has been known. They are recorded both for the sake of a greater measure of completeness and because there may be value for the non-specialist in summarizing them against the background of this narrative. Some items specialists might look for are omitted because in this case they do not apply.

It appeared in the Greenville County Council for Community Development that projects succeeded in the proportion that they were democratically planned and carried out. In terms of community development this means that every person have at least an opportunity to share in decisions in which he is interested or which affect him. The philosophy behind this of course is that the growth of persons is more important than the activities by which they grow, provided those activities are socially useful. The process of growth becomes more important than any given product. This was the basic philosophy of the staff.

Organizational implications.—It follows that any new com-

2. For a discussion of the sociological theory of community organization as it was confirmed and amended by the Greenville experiment, see C. B. Loomis, *An Experiment in Community Development with a Discussion of the Principles of Community Organization.* (Forthcoming.)

munity organization should originate within the community and not be imposed from without. The sponsoring body should be small but inclusive of the groups and organizations in the community, not omitting governmental representatives. This procedure was followed in the most successful of the local councils in Greenville County.

The executive committee of a community organization should not attempt to develop it too rapidly. The membership should be kept informed and drawn into planning and participation to the maximum possible extent. It was in this particular of policy making and program initiation that the Executive Committee of the Greenville County Council for Community Development functioned least well after the first six months. Too much time was required of busy people. Thus they largely accepted recommendations of the staff or committees or officers, sometimes uncritically, and tended really to think only when some emergency arose. In terms of a county-wide organization an executive committee composed of representatives of the area councils and county-wide groups might be more effective than a committee elected by the Council as a whole. Its membership should probably be revolving.

On the whole, standing committees proved unsatisfactory. The difficulties of the Committee on Economics and Government have been reported. The educational and social welfare committees did carry through a number of projects, some important, but they had not only staff but professional leadership. The education committee did not draw laymen into its membership. The Greenville experience seems to indicate that the best results are obtained by special committees set up to have charge of special projects for the duration of such projects. So far as possible in the course of a year each member of the organizations should have some committee assignment or other service to perform for a council.

If a community organization has an executive secretary he should make periodic reports to the executive committee and the community. If there is a staff the executive should keep it informed of the progress of the total program. The staff should meet with the executive committee periodically and of course with the whole organization. When the executive committee considers any specific project the staff member responsible should always be present.

The budget of the council should be the result of the program adopted and should be made public.

Needless to say, all staff members should be chosen not only with respect to their professional competence but also with respect to their ability to work by democratic means. Coöperation is the *sine qua non* of community organization and developments, for the participation of the members is voluntary and knows no compulsion save the members' own willingness. The mildest sort of dictation soon wrecks an enterprise of this sort whether the dictation comes from staff member or lay officer.

Program planning and action.—The program should grow out of recognized needs. If these cannot be clearly defined a study of the situation or problem should be made to serve as the basis of action. As a rule there should be definite, understandable purposes behind each survey, and laymen as well as experts, if any are available, should contribute to it. If experts are employed they should be brought in after the problem is recognized, to help analyze it and provide sources of data or help for its solution. The expert should be a resource not an action person. His advice must be integrated into the democratic process. In the planning stage even the staff member must be more of a participant observer than a director.

It is well in planning to take up first proposals that have a reasonable chance of success within a comparatively short space of time. The focusing of one community council on two difficult, long-range projects discouraged it greatly, as pointed out in Chapter V. The nearer people are to a problem the more concrete the planning is likely to be, the better its chances of success. Both because success creates a psychology of achievement and because people grow as they coöperate, more difficult projects can be taken on later. The wider relationships involved in such ventures are also the more easily seen.

Plans once made must, if at all possible, be carried all the way through. Many failures that occur are due largely to negligence in completing activities. When they are not completed, or when failures occur, the group concerned should analyze the reasons for lack of success and seek to make even a disappointing experience educative and turn it to good account. If a project is dropped for legitimate reasons, especially if it has aroused expectations in the community, the constituency should be frankly informed.

Enlarging participation.—Leaders must be constantly alert to bring new people into the work of the organization and newcomers into the membership of the community or neighborhood agency. A county council on the other hand has to operate on a delegated basis. Occasional activities that enlist many people may serve as an opportunity for enlisting new workers, but no considerable influx should be expected from such activities which should be done for their own sake.

Unsolved problems.—The positive way in which these generalizations are stated should not mislead the reader into imagining there were no unsolved problems or that the staff always knew the answers. There were many problems for which no ready answer was found. It is not always easy or even possible to be sure in advance which activities will be successful. Even when reasonable certainty exists it is sometimes difficult to lead a group to undertake these as against other more difficult jobs that look easy in the first enthusiasm of organization. When a community begins on an easy level, the shifting of the basis of activities from obvious, material improvements to more fundamental projects affecting the level of living is not an automatic thing. As noted in Chapter V this was accomplished in some of the local councils but. not in others. The explanation of the differences soon goes beyond the realm of the demonstrable into factors of tradition, leadership, and a number of similar intangibles.

Nor is there any formula for meeting difficulties inherent in deep conflict situations that may exist in a community. County Council staff members saw coöperation heal old sores but they also saw coöperation break down under the desire of officers for power, because of mistrust of the leaders selected, because of divisions along religious, occupational, or social lines and because of sheer inertia. When non-coöperation exists it must either be conquered or the worker must give up temporarily and turn attention to more fruitful areas.

General observations.—It seems quite clear from this experiment in Greenville County that some outside stimulus and probably continuing leadership is necessary for effective community organization and development. In a rural community or small city this may be furnished by a person otherwise employed who is willing to make this project his chief avocational interest. The school is often the key to such a situation if the administrator is desirous of making his institution a community school or permits a vocational or some other teacher so to do. Such a person must possess skill in leadership and faith in democratic procedure. In a city or an area as large as the average county this stimulus and leadership must come from someone professionally employed for the task.

Of all the efforts of the Greenville County Council for Community Development those in the rural areas, taken as a whole, were the most successful and of these, in the words of the Council's executive secretary, Mr. C. B. Loomis, "The Area [i.e., local community] Council idea coördinated with a developing concept of the 'Community School' holds greatest hope for the future of a creative rural life. With the school considering its task of education as extending from birth to death, with a curriculum increasingly built out of the ongoing everyday experiences of the people, and with a Council to give organizational outlet to coöperative efforts to solve community problems, the possibility of continuous individual growth to the end that the 'good life' may be more nearly achieved for all, becomes a reality."

Appendix I

Coördinator: M. C. S. Noble, Jr., 1936-37; C. B. Loomis, 1937-41.

Health: Mayo Tolman, 1936-37; Rosa Clarke, RN, 1937-39.

Government: N. P. Mitchell, 1936-41.

Social: Laura Smith Ebaugh, 1936-41; Gordon W. Blackwell, 1937-41.

Education: Ralph M. Lyon, 1936-41; Margaret C. Lyon, 1936-39; Wendell A. Norvell, 1938-41.

Arts and Crafts: Michael Seymour, 1936-37.

Recreation: Russell Bailey, 1935-36; Rachel Wells, 1938; Mell Curen, 1939; Frances Ferguson, 1939-40; Charlotte Corzine, 1940-41.

Negro: Alfred Moore, 1936-37; Cora Chapman, 1936-38; R. O. Johnson, 1938-41.

Home Demonstration Agent: Julia Stebbins, 1939-41.

Rural Librarian: Annie Porter, 1939-41.

Appendix II

Name: The name of this organization shall be the Greenville County Council for Community Development.

Purpose: The purpose is to make Greenville County a better place in which to live:

a. To inaugurate a program for community development that will attempt to coördinate the various agencies now operating in the county and make them maximally efficient; to bring individuals, both students and citizens, in close touch with the community environment and problems.

b. To use to utmost the county's assets, known and discoverable, in means and leadership, to secure the best possible life for all the residents of the county.

Membership: Membership in the Council shall be by invitation to approximately 100 representative residents of Greenville County who have demonstrated their interest and their activity in the field of community leadership.

Duties: The Council shall formulate policies and initiate programs necessary to carry out the purpose of the Council. It shall elect a chairman, vice chairman and a secretary-treasurer, annually at the regular council meeting in January. The chairman shall appoint an Executive Committee of nine, of which the elected officers shall be Ex-officio members, the Council Chairman acting as Chairman of the Executive Committee. Prior to the annual meeting the chairman shall appoint a nominating committee of three to present nominations for the above officers.

Executive Committee: The Executive Committee shall represent and be responsible to the Council for all ad-interim matters pertaining to finance, staff and committee personnel, and program.

Finance Committee: The Executive Committee shall provide for a finance committee of three whose duties shall be to prepare the budget, and to pass on all expenditures of the Council.

Advisory Committee: An Advisory Committee shall be appointed by the Executive Committee of those persons outside of Greenville County who have demonstrated their interest and their activity in the fields in which the Council's program operates, and who in the judgment of the Executive Committee would make a contribution to the Council's program.

Executive Secretary: An Executive Secretary shall be secured by the Executive Committee to act as Executive of the Council. He shall work under the authority of the Executive Committee.

Meetings: The Council shall meet on call of the Executive Committee but should meet not less than three times yearly, preferably in January, May and October.

www.ingramcontent.com/pod-product-compliance
Lightning Source LLC
Chambersburg PA
CBHW030654270326
41929CB00007B/362